Grace, Faith, and the Power of Singing

The Alma Christina Lind Swensson Story

To Curt and Joanie,
With thankfulness for our
many years of friendship, our
shared love of history, and our
journey together.

Karen A. Humphrey

Karen

Lutheran University Press

Minneapolis, Minnesota

Grace, Faith, and the Power of Singing
The Alma Christina Lind Swensson Story

Cover and interior design by Karen Walhof, Creative Advantage Design.

Cover photo by B. G. Gröndal.

Library of Congress Cataloging-in-Publication Data

Humphrey, Karen A.
  Grace, faith, and the power of singing : the Alma Christina Lind Swensson story / by Karen A. Humphrey.
     p. cm.
  ISBN 978-1-932688-72-6 (alk. paper) -- ISBN 1-932688-72-2 (alk. paper)
  1. Swensson, Alma Christina Lind, 1859-1939. 2. Church musicians--Kansas--Lindsborg--Biography. 3. Music--Kansas--Lindsborg--History and criticism. 4. Swensson, Carl Aaron, 1857-1904. 5. Lindsborg (Kan.)--Biography. 6. Lindsborg (Kan.)--Social life and customs. I. Title.
  ML420.S9655H85 2012
  780.92--dc23
  [B]
                                             2012007743

Lutheran University Press, PO Box 390759. Minneapolis, MN 55439
www.lutheranupress.org
Manufactured in the United States of America

To the memory of Alma Christina Lind Swensson,
to church musicians who enrich worship and change lives,
to those who serve others with dignity and grace,
and to all the parsonage women—wives, mothers, and daughters—
who build communities of love and justice.

Table of Contents

Introduction

For eight years, I walked in the footsteps of Alma Christina Lind Swensson in Lindsborg, Kansas, where she lived sixty years of her life. I, too, was the wife of the pastor of Bethany Lutheran Church, and I always believed I was one of the inheritors of the great work Alma accomplished for the church, the college, and the community. My husband was called to be the pastor of Bethany Lutheran Church in 1998. The church was founded by the Swedish immigrant Pastor Olof Olsson in 1869, and was served by Pastor Carl Aaron Swensson from 1879 to 1904. My own work in Lindsborg was for Bethany College, founded by Swensson in the sacristy of Bethany Lutheran Church in 1881.

Carl Aaron Swensson's name and image are everywhere—there is a plaster bust of him in every college building and one in the church, too, and an Italian marble statue is the centerpiece of the college campus. Carl was president of the Kansas Conference of the Augustana Lutheran Synod, served in the Kansas State House of Representatives, a member of the speaker's bureau for McKinley and Roosevelt, the editor of several newspapers, wrote opinion pieces, devotional books, and toured Sweden twice in the 1890s. When he came home he published a doorstop of a volume about his experiences, travelogues of his journeys that were widely read throughout Sweden and Swedish America. He wrote in superlatives—in glowing terms to attract people to his community and capture his vision. He was a gifted orator, one who could take in his audience, convince farmers suffering from drought, depression, grasshoppers, low prices, and devastating windstorms that tomorrow would be better—*i morgan blir det bättre*—and help them see a future that they could never have imagined.

Carl Aaron Swensson was called "The Colossus of the Plains." One of our neighbors, who was ninety-two and had lived in the community all her life, told the story of a class of Sunday school children in Lindsborg who were learning the creation story from Genesis. The kind teacher asked her eager students, "Who created the heavens and the earth?" A little boy raised his hand and said, "Why, it was Dr. Carl Aaron Swensson!"

At Bethany Lutheran Church and Bethany College, there are also portraits of a calm, serene woman, her white hair softly arranged to reveal a high forehead. She wears a black dress with a jewel neckline, a jacket with silk lapels, and a black velvet ribbon encircling her neck. Her metal-rimmed glasses are round and bridge a rather broad nose. There are slight dimples as she smiles. This is Alma Christina Lind Swensson—Mrs. Rev. Dr. Swensson, as she was called. She was the church organist and choir director for forty years, and over the winter of 1881 and 1882 taught a choir of farmers, shopkeepers, and homemakers still speaking Swedish the words and music of Handel's glorious oratorio, The *Messiah*. She herself sang the soprano solos when The *Messiah* was presented for the first time on March 28, 1882. Alma also served on the music faculty of Bethany College. She gave birth to two daughters and raised them in the public eye of the parsonage. She kept house, welcomed guests, and kept things going while Carl was on his many, many travels. And later in her life, after Carl's untimely death, she touched the world.

There are snippets of Alma's life story here and there in the published histories of Lindsborg, Bethany College, and Bethany Church. In this volume, I hope to stitch together a whole story of her life.

Beginning at Broddarp

Broddarp is a wide spot on a plain in southwestern Sweden, in Västergötland. The village of some 115 residents sits in the middle of a triangle anchored by larger and well-known cities of Falköping, Ulricehamn, and Herrljunga. The church at Broddarp is the cultural center of the community where the children eagerly present a Saint Lucia pageant each December 13.[1] The sanctuary, then, is illuminated by a crown of live candles worn by young Lucia in remembrance of the legendary saint who, it is said, brought food to the poor and suffering during a famine in Sweden.

This church at Broddarp, built in the late nineteenth century, replaced a twelfth-century stone church that held the relics of *Den Helige Botulf* (St. Botulf), the seventh century English patron saint of travelers and various aspects of farming. A photograph of the old stone church reveals that there was a separate wooden bell tower. At sundown on Saturday, the bell could be heard ringing in the Sabbath. Broddarp's *gamla kyrka* and bell tower were dismantled in favor of the newer sanctuary. But in the graveyard still today, stand two ancient, weather-beaten stones with engraved crosses. So important are they to the cultural story of the area that they are marked with "RAÄ," a sign of protection from the *Riksantikvarrieämbetet*—the Swedish National Heritage Board.[2] The life journey of Alma Christina Lind Swensson begins at this place, Broddarp.[3] She was the first daughter of an old soldier named Johan Lind and his second wife.

Johan was an *indelte*, an old time "blue boy" from the reigns of Carl XIV Johan, Oscar I, and Carl XV. The *indelte* was a farmer-soldier who lived on a large estate and, for his service in the military, received the use of two to four acres of land, a small house, and provisions of food and payment each year. His required service was to be away from the land and his family when his regiment assembled for maneuvers for two weeks every summer. He wore the uniform of the crown, and his motto was: Fear God, honor the king, do right towards every man, serve the country. After those two weeks, the soldier was free the rest of the year to farm, work in the forest, and do carpentry or other labor that would help support his family. If war should come, he was obliged to defend his country.

Johan Lind's first wife, Maria Kristina Larsdotter, died after fourteen years of marriage and five children, all who died in infancy. It was not unusual then for a widower to marry his wife's sister, and so he married Fredrika Larsdotter. Their first child, Ephraim, was born, strong and healthy, on June 18, 1857.

During the summer of 1858, while on maneuvers with a large assembly of military forces training in the presence of Crown Prince Carl, Johan's name was called. Johan stepped forward as ordered. He was tall and slender with a dignified bearing. His captain announced before all the assembled troops that Johan Lind would be awarded the Medal of the Sword for faithful and capable service to the king. It was June 24th, *Midsommar's* Day, and meadows around the troops were bursting with colorful wildflowers. Proudly wearing his medal, Johan came home to resume the life of a farmer and carpenter. He became a highly respected member of the community.[4]

Johan was a skilled craftsman—a builder of sturdy, functional, yet beautiful tables, desks, chairs, and bookshelves. This was the work he loved during the long Swedish winter nights and into the sun-drenched summer days until it was time to report again for maneuvers. In the summer of 1859 he returned home to the work of the farm and shop, taking great pleasure in young Ephraim. Johan was forty-five-years-old, and Fredrika was pregnant again.

On December 11, 1859 Fredrika gave birth to a daughter. The very next day, on the eve of Saint Lucia, Johan brought their baby through the cold, dark winter to the old stone Broddarp church where she was baptized Alma Christina at the ancient font. The church register, although difficult to read, shows the witnesses were Anderson and Signe Gusta, farmers from Grondal. Alma is the last child born and baptized in 1859 according to the Broddarp parish record.[5]

Now the days of Christmas were approaching—the time when women were in charge of butchering, brewing, candlemaking, baking, and intensive cleaning. But Fredrika, recovering from the birth of her child, may have taken time to rest and ponder more deeply the meaning of Christmas that year. She may have felt a closer identity with Mary, mother of the Christ child and the same hope a mother feels with every new baby—the promise of a future yet unseen. In the dark morning hours of December 25, Alma stirred in her mother's arms at the sound of the Broddarp church bell ringing from its wooden tower announcing *Julotta*—the early Christmas morning matins.

As she grew little Alma experienced the curiosity and joy of discovery during each season. She followed her mother through her responsibilities and daily routines—to the garden for planting potatoes, turnips, and carrots in the spring; to the pasture where the little girl picked summer flowers; to the field in late summer, harvesting flax and oats; in the small kitchen where Fredrika prepared their daily bread; to the barn were her mother milked the cow twice each day. She splashed in the water while her mother bent over the washtub scrubbing clothes. There was the season of spinning and weaving, the season of sewing clothes and mending by window light or lamp light, the season of putting up preserves of meat and fruit and vegetables, the deep cleaning season before Christmas.

Alma Christina Lind would not necessarily inherit the solely labor-intensive work of her mother's and her grandmothers' people, for Alma was born to an era of promise, of breakthroughs for women, and of opportunities for little girls to grow into more fulfilling lives than their mothers imagined.

At the same time, in other parts of Scandinavia, little girls named Karin Bergöö (b, 1859), Anna Brøndum (b. 1859), Agnes Mathilde Wergeland (b. 1857), and Selma Lagerlöf (b. 1858), would grow up to receive recognition for their expressions in fine art, literature, education, and decorative arts in ways that women had not experienced before. Selma Lagerlöf, whose father was also a soldier, would win a Nobel Prize for literature. Karin Bergöö, would create such an atmosphere for the home that all of the world would long for and value Swedish family life depicted in the paintings of her husband, Carl Larsson. Anna Brøndum would become an artist and the central figure in the world of Nordic impressionism at the Danish art colony of Skagen with her husband, Michael Ancher. Agnes Mathilde Wergeland would become the first of her countrywomen to earn a Ph.D. Alma Christina Lind would use her gifts to create an environment of culture, education, hospitality, service, and music that would have a significant influence on generations of lives. But Alma, her mother and father, and her brother Ephraim first had to endure the hardships of leaving home and emigrating to America.

Over to Illinois

Sweden was gripped by "America fever" in the 1850s. The great emigration had begun in 1845, and by the time it was over, almost ninety years later, twenty to twenty-five percent of all Swedes who were alive in those years lived in America.[6]

Letters from earlier emigrants, the so-called "America letters," fueled the interest of peasants who were living marginal lives or who longed to be landowners instead of tenant farmers. The America letters painted an attractive portrait of opportunity in the United States. Mary Jonson Stephenson was one who wrote to her family still in the Edshult parish in Småland from her home in New Sweden, Iowa, August 2, 1864:

> Our new home has many advantages over the old one, and I like it much better. We have a good level road to church, and the distance is no greater. I sell butter and eggs to a man who calls every other week. I believe I have sold twenty dollars' worth of eggs, besides considerable butter. We have four cows. We sheared six sheep. I have twenty-four pounds of wool. I have begun to spin, and I intend to weave thirty yards of cloth warped with wool.[7]

Johan Lind received letters from a brother-in-law in Illinois where a goodly number of Swedes had already settled, and so conversations about the possibility of going to America began in the Lind household. But how would this old soldier, loyal to the crown, leave Sweden? He would never desert his king. He had to become honorably free from the military by resigning his commission, and to do that, he needed to purchase a small farm of his own.

Until the appropriate measures could be taken, Johan and Fredrika studied published information about preparing to leave home. One of the most popular and informative guides was written by the Rev. Erland Carlsson, a Swedish Lutheran pastor in America of the Augustana Evangelical Lutheran Synod, established by immigrant Swedish Lutherans in 1860. Carlsson's guide concerned both temporal and spiritual matters. He advised on items that should be packed in an emigrant's trunk for the long journey:

> Implements and other things ought not to be taken along at all; or at least only the fewest possible. Good dress clothes and work clothes, two and at the most three outfits together with good bedclothes as well as a quantity of linen—this is all except that each emigrant ought to be equipped with flannel or wool to wear nearest his body. This is the greatest importance not only for the sea voyage, but also for residence here. . . . Likewise, emigrants ought not to forget to provide themselves with a quantity of good Swedish books because such can not be bought here without ordering them from Sweden. In addition to the Bible, Luther's *Postils*, and some other good devotional book, for example, Arndt's *True Christianity*, they may take along psalmbooks, catechisms, Barth's *Bible History*, and A.B.C. books.[8]

Eventually, Johan was able to purchase a farm. When it was sold, he honorably resigned his military commission. In addition, he applied for and received the required release from the Church of Sweden for himself and his family. When all the formal papers were signed, the house cleaned, and the last items packed into their trunk, final good-byes were said to the community at Broddarp. Fredrika and Johan then took young Ephraim and four-year-old Alma Christina by the hand, climbed into a horse-drawn wagon, and left their home for good on May 5, 1864. They made their way to the Swedish seacoast port of Göteborg where they waited a week for a ship that would take them to Hamburg, Germany. After five weeks in Hamburg the family boarded the ship *Nord* that would sail them across the Atlantic Ocean for their new life in a new world. Their ultimate destination was Andover, Illinois.

The *Nord* sailed into New York harbor on August 24, 1864. Through the vast, confusing city with a cacophony of voices and languages, they had to find a way to reach Andover, halfway across the American continent.

Often there were agents providing assistance to emigrants, and perhaps someone helped the family purchase tickets for the next leg of their journey. Presumably, they took a boat up the Hudson River, through the Erie Canal, and around the Great Lakes to Chicago. From Chicago, a canal boat would bring them to Peru, Illinois. Then at last Johan, Fredrika, Ephraim, and Alma climbed into a covered wagon that brought them to their final stop—Andover, Henry County—to America's middle west and a community of immigrants sharing the experience of adapting to a new country.

The village of Andover had been organized in 1835 by the Rev. Ithamar Pillsbury, a Presbyterian minister who had a vision of creating a new New Haven, Connecticut—a place for education, commerce, and faith. The first Swedish immigrant, Sven Nelson, arrived in 1840, and saw the potential of the vast rolling prairie as farmland. As it turned out, Nelson had the better vision. The virgin prairie grass, when turned, revealed the richest soil on the face of the earth. Hundreds of Swedish immigrants eventually followed Nelson, all eager to acquire farmland.

But Andover also became a place of faith. Standing at the center of the community was a small chapel built in 1850, thanks to a gift from the beloved Swedish opera star Jenny Lind. The little church—simple, foursquare, plain, and built of common white clapboard—was to have a steeple. But in 1853 a terrible cholera epidemic struck the Swedish settlement, and wood that was to build a steeple was used to build coffins instead. The basement of the partially finished chapel had to be used for an infirmary.

By the time the Lind family arrived, the chapel, which could hold 300 people, was now so crowded for worship services that a hole was cut in the floor and a railing built around it so that those seated in the basement could hear the pastor and take part in the singing.[9] Plans were underway to build a new sanctuary, and subscriptions for the project had already begun. The new church would be made of 500,000 bricks, and every male member of the congregation would be required to make their share. Johan Lind, skilled at carpentry, may have helped build the new edifice that would become a cathedral-like structure, marked by a steeple 136 feet into the air.

The pastor of the Andover Lutheran congregation was the Rev. Jonas Swensson, a native of Våthult's parish, Småland, Sweden, who came to

Andover in 1858 from the Hessel Valley, Pennsylvania.[10] He brought his wife, Marie, and their son, Carl Aaron, born in 1857.

It seems almost certain that the pastor's son, now nine years old, would have noticed the slender girl with wide eyes whose name was Alma Christina. Perhaps they played together after worship services or watched their fathers discuss the plans for the new sanctuary or sang in the children's choir. Perhaps they processed into the sanctuary together at *Julotta*,[11] singing the festive hymns their parents would have known in Sweden: *Var hälsad, sköna morgonstund* ("How Brightly Shines the Morning Star"), and the gentle children's hymn *När juldagsmorgon glimmar* ("When Christmas Morn is Dawning"). Carl and Alma, along with all Swedish immigrant children growing up on the prairies and forests of Illinois, Minnesota, Wisconsin, Iowa, and on the plains of Kansas and Nebraska, would have been taught these hymns and would treasure them all their lives.

If Alma and Carl had become young friends, it was only for a brief time. Shortly after New Year's Day 1866, Johan and Fredrika loaded a sledge with their earthly belongings, wrapped their children Ephraim, Alma, and new baby Herman in the warmest clothes they could find, and made their way north across the snowy, dormant fields of gently rolling hills to Moline, an up-and-coming industrial town on the Mississippi River some twenty-six miles north. The bustling town of factories provided the hope of jobs for the influx of immigrants. Many were attracted to Moline to work in the Deere plow factory or at any number of flour mills, feed mills, lumber mills, and manufacturers of steam engines and furniture.

Johan and Fredrika found a house for their family on Henry Street, on the same block as the Swedish Lutheran Church, founded in 1850 by the Rev. Lars Paul Esbjorn.[12] The church was the heart of the well-established Swedish immigrant district. Across the street and down the block, merchants with the names of Wickstrom, Colson, Lundvall, Fjellander, Swanson, and Lundquist had set up grocery stores, a tailor shop, jewelry and hardware stores, a meat market, and flour and feed stores.[13]

The church building, constructed in 1851, was not unlike the chapel at Andover, and soon it, too, would be expanded to accommodate the growing membership. Right next to the church the congregation built a parish schoolhouse where the Lind children attended with most of the other children of the neighborhood. Instructed by Swedish-speaking teachers, the children learned Bible history, Luther's catechism, arithmetic, history, Swedish grammar, and English. But each school day opened with singing and devotions which were held in the church. There was a melodeon, also known as a cabinet organ, to accompany the school children. And it is most likely here, during those daily morning devotions, that Alma's gift for music was discovered. She may have had a clear, sweet soprano voice with a good ear for the melody line. Perhaps she lingered at the melodeon after morning devotions or came after school to take a closer look at the instrument and how it made music to accompany the singing. Perhaps one of her teachers, Mr. Törnvall, Mr. Söderling, Mr. Rydholm, or Mr. Nordling, noticed how the singing sparked Alma's curiosity—how voices came together to sound as one, how uplifting the hymns could be, how the melodeon could support the voices around her. However it happened, church music became the course of Alma's life at a young, tender age.

Johan and Fredrika somehow saw to it that their oldest daughter could pursue this interest. Her parents may have spared her tedious household chores so she would have more time to practice scales and chords on the melodeon. But more likely she finished helping her mother and then was free to practice her musical lessons. Her abilities certainly must have developed rapidly, to such a degree that Alma became the organist at the Swedish Lutheran Church in 1871. She was twelve years old. Congregational minutes show that she was paid $15.00 for the period of May 1, 1871 to May 1, 1872.[14] She held the position for eight years.

When she was fourteen, while organist of the church, Alma studied Luther's catechism with her confirmation class led by their pastor, A. G. Setterdahl.[15] The class of forty members was confirmed in the spring of 1875 in the rite of the Swedish Lutheran Church. Alma, like many other members of her class, had been baptized at an ancient font in her home parish in Sweden. Now she knelt for her confirmation vows at a new altar in a new church, far from Broddarp. The liturgy, the hymns, and the promises the confirmands made were the same, brought from the Church of Sweden.

It was common fact that most young immigrant girls ended their formal education after confirmation. But Alma's parents, perhaps most of all her mother, wanted Alma to have an education beyond eighth grade. By 1874, Fredrika had given birth to three more children: Anna Nora in

1868, Jenny in 1872, Hilma in 1874. All of them were strong and healthy babies, and with Ephraim, Alma, and Herman, there were six children to care for and nurture. Her parents could have told Alma that, as the oldest daughter, her place should be at home helping care for her siblings and keeping house—scrubbing floors, washing clothes in vats of boiling water, then scrubbing them on a washboard, mending clothes by lamp light, keeping a garden, preparing meals, baking bread, washing dishes, weaving rugs, dipping candles, churning butter, making soap, perhaps raising chickens in the backyard, along with milking a cow kept on the property in a small barn. But there was something about young Alma that caused her parents to see that her education should be continued. And so she enrolled in the Moline Public School, outside of the Swedish community. She was about to stretch her mind and all her abilities.

Early in the morning, Alma would leave her home on Henry Street, walk past the church as it caught the morning light, and make her way three blocks north to Lynde Street. Now she would turn east, walk past the Congregational Church, then propel herself up the hill to the Moline School on Dean Street. Built on a bluff overlooking the city and the winding Mississippi River, the school was a magnificent design of the Second French Empire period. There were cement stairs students ascended from the street—several sets of stairs—to walk up to the school. It was as if the idea of education was lifted above the drone of city life and smoldering factory smokestacks. At this school, with its tall windows and high ceilings, students were given even the physical sense that education was a noble pursuit, an aspiration to be reached by the young people who approached the school door each day.

Alma's schoolmates were not from her neighborhood. Her confirmation class at the Swedish Lutheran Church included four Andersons, four Johnsons, five Larsons, three Petersons, and assorted Swensons, Ericsons, Carlsons, and Jacobsons. But her schoolmates had the names of Ainsworth, Huntoon, Knowles, Kerns, and Joslyn. They were the children of Moline's founding families. May Dow's family, for example, came from Maryland and Vermont where her mother studied Latin, mathematics, and French, and her father was a classical scholar who taught in Chicago before moving the family to Moline. Minnie Stephens was the daughter of George Stephens, the founder of the Moline Plow Company. Her moth-

Alma Christina Lind,perhaps at her confirmation or graduation.

er's ancestors were the Hopkins who founded the city of Providence, Rhode Island. Another ancestor was Stephen Hopkins, who signed the Declaration of Independence. Lillie Swan's father came to Moline in 1857, dead broke, but his investments in the Moline Union Agricultural Works made him a wealthy man.[16] Alma's father, Johan, was an old Swedish soldier decorated by the crown prince, but now a self-employed carpenter. Alma's surname appears to be the only Scandinavian name on the class roster, and Alma the only immigrant among the fourteen members of her class. Swedish was her first language. She was just beginning to learn English.

But the gift of music helped Alma find her path in her new school. The school introduced singing exercises at the beginning of the school year, and on May 28, 1875, Alma Lind sang a duet, a German song, "Good Night," with a Miss Quinn as the finale of the end-of-year program presented to the public.[17]

If 1875 was a turning point in the education of Alma Christina Lind, the year was also a turning point in the history of Moline and its neighboring city, Rock Island. The Augustana College and Seminary moved its small campus from Paxton, Illinois, to Rock Island. The professors and students of Augustana College would make Moline's Swedish Lutheran Church their place of worship.

Among the students who would become a member of the church was none other than Carl Aaron Swensson, the pastor's son from Andover. Since Alma had last seen him, Carl's life was marked by the tragic, untimely death of his father, Jonas, at Christmas 1873. His mother, Maria, died just eight months later. After their parents' death, two of Carl's youngest siblings were cared for in a children's home and another brother was left to be on his own. Following his father's wishes, Carl enrolled at Augustana College, and he now would be in the first graduating class.

And so Alma and Carl met again at church. Both seemed to be young people of great determination, intent on making their way with faith and service to the church at the center of their lives. By day Alma went to public school; by night she studied her lessons, helped with family responsibilities, and rehearsed the hymns and liturgy she played for worship.

The liturgy of the Swedish Lutheran Church was based on liturgical music prepared by the reformer Olavus Petri in 1531, which was based on Gregorian chant from the Middle Ages.[18] Carried by clergy and lay people from their home parishes in Sweden, the Sunday morning worship in Swedish-American churches continued an unbroken tradition of liturgical singing from the sixteenth century.[19] When the Lutheran immigrants gathered in homes, they sang the liturgy and many of the hymns by heart. With an organ in a church setting, this liturgy required four-part chordal movement.

The organist set the tone for worship with the opening hymn and then became a full participant in the liturgy as she played the pastor's intonation as well as the congregational responses. After the appropriate opening hymn, the pastor sang, accompanied by the organist, "*Helig, helig, helig är Herren Sebaot. Hela jorden är full av hans härlighet.*"[20] Those who remember this old Swedish liturgy used to say that it brought them into the very holy presence of God. At such a young age, it was remarkable that Alma could enhance the liturgy that demanded dignity and skillful playing.[21]

The Moline congregation grew in membership each year, and with that grew the magnitude of duties of the young church organist. In 1877, when Alma was eighteen years of age, the church recorded 114 baptisms, ten weddings, thirty-six funerals, in a congregation of 919 adults. Each service required hymns and special music in addition to the Sunday liturgy.

The congregation expressed appreciation to their young organist in the minutes of the annual meetings:

> It has hereby been decided that the congregation acknowledge with gratitude Miss Alma Lind's merit as organist along with the attentiveness and belief she has displayed.[22]

In the autumn of 1877, Alma began her senior year at Moline High School under the leadership of a new principal, Mary Keyes, who carried a passion for education for women and men.[23] Alma's class met weekly at the residence of one of its members for extra study of English literature. "They are struggling for proficiency in this valuable branch of education," the Rock Island *Daily Union* noted in early 1878. On Class Day, Friday, May 3, the young women and one young man of the senior class were on stage to give presentations to the public. Allie Brett's declamation was entitled "Through Death to Life," and Alma and May Dow played a piano duet, "Caliph of Baghdad" from the comic opera by François-Adrien Boieldieu. Near the end of the program Alma joined Allie Brett in George Cooper's popular ballad of the day, "Down Among the Lilies," and the program ended with the class singing "Sweet By and By." The *Daily Union* reported after the program, "It is the most promising class that has graduated here for years."[24] A public examination of the graduates was held the following week, followed by the graduation exercises where Alma read her essay, "Icebergs." She argued that "ignorance of every form is the iceberg of society, chilling everything good that comes within its reach and wrecking the courageous mariner who dares to go upon the sea of knowledge in search of wisdom." "The production was well received and evidently greatly appreciated," the Rock Island *Daily Union* reporter noted.[25] A reception in honor of the Class was attended by 150 people in the home of C. R. Ainsworth—one of the prominent businessmen of Moline. Alma was the first member of her family to graduate from high school.

The year of Alma's graduation also marked a significant year at the Swedish Lutheran Church. A new sanctuary was under construction on Henry Street to accommodate the congregation which was growing beyond anything Pastor Esbjorn could have imagined.

But in March of 1878, Pastor Setterdahl announced to the congregation that he was not well, and would go home to Sweden to regain his health. Serving as interim pastor would be the Rev. Olof Olsson who recently moved to Illinois from Bethany Lutheran Church and the Swedish settlement of Lindsborg, Kansas, some 600 miles to the west, on the edge of the Great Plains. Pastor Olsson's family included his oldest daughter, Anna, born in Värmland, Sweden. She might have shared stories with Alma and other young people of the congregation about her life on the frontier at Lindsborg. "I was scared," Anna said.

Lindsborg, Kansas

Bright, clear sky over a plain so wide that the rim of the heavens cut down on it around the entire horizon. . . . Bright, clear sky, to-day, to-morrow, and for all time to come (Ole Rolvaag).

The moon is the closest of the celestial bodies. But no amount of walking will get you any closer to it. The prairie, in this respect, resembles the moon. The essential feature of the prairie is its horizon, which you can neither walk to nor touch (Paul Gruchow).

. . . but a prairie man looks at a square foot and sees a universe; ten or twenty flowers and grasses, heights, heads, colors, shades, configurations, bearded, rough, smooth, simple, elegant. When a cloud passes over the sun, colors shift, like a child's kaleidoscope" (Bill Holm).

The native prairies were breathtakingly beautiful, but there were many things to scare Anna Olsson, who lived at Lindsborg, Kansas, from 1869 to 1876. When she was a grown woman, this daughter of the prairie published her impressions of her childhood on the edge of the vast American Great Plains. She wrote "I'm scairt."[26] Anna remembered a buffalo stampede destroying the roof of a sod house, snakes falling from the ceiling of a dugout into a bowl of soup, a skunk creeping out from under the pulpit during a Sunday morning service, a wolf howling at the door, the grasshoppers of 1874 that destroyed the crops and dashed peoples hopes, persistent drought, blistering heat, constant winds. At the early organization of the First Swedish Agricultural Company, someone suggested that it would be dangerous to locate in Kansas, then called the

Great American Desert, because it rarely rained there. Company chairman John Ferm answered, "If God is going to let us settle in Kansas, he will give us rain."[27]

The Kansas landscape could not have reminded Anna or any of the settlers of the landscape they left in Sweden. But the story of Lindsborg, the little town in the Smoky Valley of central Kansas, really begins among the birch trees, coniferous forests, shimmering lakes, and gurgling streams in the storybook province of Värmland.[28]

To be more precise, the story of Lindsborg begins at the Noretorp parsonage in the Sunnemo parish, and the growing unease, disenchantment, and concern Pastor Olof Olsson had with the Swedish State Church. Olsson—young, dynamic, pious, and a gifted preacher—and his wife Anna Lisa Jonsdotter had begun conversations about the possibilities there might be for their devout and pietistic faith in the United States—perhaps even to start a new church there.

Olof started an exchange of letters with Pastor T. N. Hasselquist, president of the Augustana Synod. A scouting party that included one of Olsson's closest friends, C. R. Carlson, sailed to America to find land. The First Swedish Agricultural Company of McPherson County, Kansas, was established on April 17, 1868, and acquired thousands of acres of land in McPherson and Saline counties.[29] This is where Olof and Anna Lisa would establish a new church without the influence of the state. The decision had been made.

In order to move to America, Olsson had to apply to the Karlstad Diocese for permission to leave Sunnemo and the Church of Sweden. He stated in his request that he did not wish to resign his call because he would serve the Swedish church in America. The diocese ". . . took this request under consideration but found itself unable to give its approval." Olsson then had to write to King Carl XV, who granted "freedom from service in the Church of Sweden with the obligation that he should resume his service in the Karlstad Diocese upon his return to the fatherland after completing his work among Lutheran congregations in America." Permission from the king came in March 1869.[30] In the meantime some 200 men, women, and children had begun preparations to follow Olsson to Kansas.

On Ascension Day, May 6, 1869, Pastor Olof Olsson conducted his last service at the Sunnemo Church. Almost 150 years later, the suggestion was made that Pastor Olsson deliberately chose Ascension Day to preach his last sermon so that the people who stayed in Sweden and the people who would join Pastor Olsson on this voyage to America could feel and understand the powerful sense of separation, yet the word of God would unite them always.[31] After the last worship service at the Sunnemo Church, Olof, Anna Lisa, and their three-year-old daughter Anna walked through the quiet cemetery and stopped at an iron cross under birch trees marking the grave of their daughter and sister, Maria, who was born at Noretorp on Christmas Day 1867 and died on June 18, 1868—almost at Midsommar.[32] This moment was their final goodbye.

Though Anna Lisa was leaving her homeland and her way of life, she must have been thankful that her larger family had decided to join the journey to America. Making the difficult move with them was her mother, Maria, a younger sister, Britta, and her half-brothers and half-sister, Carl, Anders, Erik, and Lovisa. Olof's parents, Olof and Britta Olsson, and his younger brother, Carl, would also go along. But even with so many family members leaving Sweden with her, Anna Lisa would always long for the beauty of Värmland. The word often used among the immigrants, especially among women, was *hemlängtan*—home longing.[33]

Their journey across the Atlantic and to the center of the United States took seven weeks. The Olssons, their family, and the entire party arrived at the little Swedish settlement in McPherson County on June 27, 1869. The nearest post office was twenty miles away. The distinguishing geographic feature of the region was a butte formed of Dakota sandstone rising more than 300 feet above the valley floor. It is alleged that Francisco Vasquez de Coronado and his soldiers climbed the butte in 1554 hoping to see Quiveria, but did not, and so turned back to Mexico.

In the shadow of Coronado's butte, the Swedish settlers built a twelve-by-fourteen foot dwelling for the pastor's family. On Sundays, the settlers gathered for worship in each other's homes with Pastor Olsson leading the familiar Lutheran liturgy. The church was organized at the *Bolagshuset*, the Swedish Land Company's community building, on August 19, 1869. The congregation was named Bethany, after the biblical village where Jesus gathered with his friends, Mary, Martha, and Lazarus.[34]

The congregation officially organized now, Olof Olsson had another task before him, one that he loved. Before entering the seminary, the beloved preacher, teacher, and friend was trained to be a church musician. He had studied with Anders Fredrik Sedström, the choirmaster, cantor, and organist at Fredsberg in Västergötland, who was a graduate of the Academy of Music in Stockholm. Olof had been tutored daily in harmony, singing, and organ, and he deeply believed in the importance of music to the worship service. Now on the Kansas prairie, he brought the best singers together as a choir (Anna Lisa was one of them), and with a tuning fork and numbering system that he devised, he taught his choir to read music and to sing four-part harmony.[35]

And all during the autumn, on this flat prairie valley, a sanctuary was built by the hands of volunteers. They located the church on a slight rise in the landscape near the center of Section 7. The walls were dark ochre sandstone, brought by horse-drawn wagons from nearby bluffs. Blocks of sod were cut and stacked on the gable ends. The roof was made of slough grass, laced to the structural poles. On each side, three small windows allowed some light. There was a dirt floor, no ceiling; rough-hewn planks propped up on cottonwood tree stumps served as pews. The altar, a table made by immigrant Olof Erickson,[36] was placed so that the congregation faced east. The humble prairie sanctuary was thirty-six by thirty-four feet, and it was ready for *Julotta*, Christmas Day, 1869. But a roaring prairie blizzard kept everyone at home.

In a week's time the prairie was quiet again, and the congregation came to their church for the first worship service on New Year's Day, 1870. Pastor Olsson led the choir as it sang out across the valley of the Smoky Hill River. Their anthem was *"Stäm in i änglers chor"* (Join in the angel's choir).[37] The melody and harmony are to the tune Thesaurus Musicus, London 1744, known to generations of Americans as "My Country 'tis of Thee." A choir had begun the new year, and the settlers at Lindsborg began a love affair with choral singing.

The small sanctuary on the prairie served the burgeoning congregation only a few years. A new church, this one near the village, was built by the members themselves of the same dark ochre native sandstone. The new sanctuary measured sixty-five by forty feet, with six tall, narrow windows on each side, and two similar narrow windows on either side of the front door. And directly above the door, they placed a round window. The sacristy itself was fourteen feet long, fourteen feet wide, and ten feet high. An Estey reed organ was purchased to support the congregational singing and the choir. The new Bethany Church sanctuary was second in size only to the churches in Chicago and Rockford, which had been established years earlier by Swedish Lutheran immigrants.[38] The church was completed on November 28, 1874, and the first worship service was held on Sunday, December 6. Olsson, who served as organist and choirmaster as well as the pastor of the congregation, played and sang "*Här en källa rinner,*" number 285 in the beloved Hemlandsånger.[39] The dedication of the new church was held during a meeting of the Kansas Conference in Lindsborg the following November, and Olsson conducted a large choir for the occasion.[40]

Many natural disasters tried the faith and courage of the Bethany congregation—tornadoes, prairie fires, blizzards, the plague of grasshoppers. The greatest threat, however, was not the natural disasters, but the controversy of the early 1870s on the doctrinal issue of atonement. The church grievously split—old friends were alienated, families divided.[41] The difficulties were heart breaking, for Olof and Anna Lisa had hoped to create a place of peace, piety, and devout service to God.

In 1876, Olof Olsson was granted a leave of absence, in part to recover his health, which had suffered because of the controversy. He also began to make plans to become a professor at Augustana Theological Seminary, still at Paxton, Illinois, the following academic year. Daughter Anna Olsson remembered this in her memoir. "Now we must say goodbye to Lindsborg," Anna wrote. "We are going to move . . . .we are going to a place called Illinois. Papa will be a teacher of older boys in a big red schoolhouse, bigger than a church. . . . Everyone is so sad, since everyone loves Papa and Mama, and Papa and Mama love everyone, too. . . . Mama is crying. She does not want to move away from Lindsborg. . . . So many friends come to our house and all of them look so sad."[42]

Before leaving Bethany Church, Pastor Olof Olsson promised the congregation that he would send the best and the brightest seminarian to be his successor.[43]

The Best and the Brightest

When Pastor Olof Olsson arrived at Augustana College, one of his first assignments was to raise money for both college and seminary. He needed a student to travel with him exemplary of the young men training to be Lutheran pastors. The student, who also became his office assistant, was Carl Aaron Swensson. In 1877 Carl accompanied Olsson on a tour by the Augustana Silver Cornet Band to congregations in Kansas' Smoky Valley, including Bethany Church. After a band concert and a twilight prayer service on Coronado Heights, Olsson recalled for the Augustana students the stories of the founding of Lindsborg.[44] The young musicians must have been mesmerized by the adventures of the place still on the edge of the frontier.

During the tour, Olsson assigned Carl to preach at Bethany Church, his former congregation still filled with friends from Sweden. Members of the congregation were dazzled by the booming voice of Carl's oratory and his self-assurance. He was called to be the pastor of the church, even before he was ordained.[45] But Carl had two more years of seminary, and so he returned to Illinois.

By the autumn of 1878, the new sanctuary of the Swedish Lutheran congregation at Moline had a cathedral's presence. The sanctuary had five aisles; eventually a complete U-shaped balcony would be wrapped from one side of the altar to the other. The setting was both majestic and worshipful for the congregation now numbering 1,600. On October 13, 1878, the first service was held in the new sanctuary with interim Pastor Olof Olsson officiating. Very likely, he and Alma Lind worked together to prepare a festive occasion. Olsson would have been impressed with the skill and ability of the young organist and musician. Perhaps it was Olsson who encouraged the romance between Carl and Alma. He knew that if the Bethany congregation needed Carl's leadership, they would thrive with the musical gifts Alma brought to the equation. Together they would bring life and energy to the Lindsborg community.[46]

Carl Aaron Swensson was ordained into the ministry of the Lutheran Church June 27, 1879, during the Augustana Synod Convention at Immanuel Lutheran Church, Chicago. He was twenty-two years old, and he now moved to Lindsborg to take up his ministry. On July 27 he was installed as pastor of Bethany Lutheran Church by Dr. T. N. Hasselquist, president of the Augustana Synod. The *Lindsborg Localist* reported, "The spacious church edifice on North Main Street was not able to contain all the people who assembled there on the day of his installation. His career promises to be one of great usefulness in this community." This would prove to be an understatement.

The newly installed pastor was already taking steps to establish a high school that would be associated with the church. At the church's annual meeting December 30, 1879, a resolution was adopted that of "the money received for the sale of land in town owned by the congregation, one half be placed in a building fund for the erection of a Lutheran school here, and the other half be placed in a church building fund."[47]

When the Lindsborg community celebrated Independence Day in July 1880, Carl was chosen to deliver an address following the oration by Kansas Governor John P. St. John. Carl's speech was aimed specifically for the great Swedish audience of the town on the prairie, just eleven years from settlement. The *Localist* stated he "was a fine young man of finished education, a fine physique, a splendid voice, an earnest speaker."[48] It seems he had won over both church and community with his eloquence, drive, and style. While others were proclaiming his speaking powers and his energy, Carl may have been thinking to himself, "Wait until they meet Alma."

Their wedding date was set: Wednesday, September 15, 1880, in Moline at the Swedish Lutheran Church. All during the day, Alma's friends decorated the church with flowers for the ceremony. In front of the altar, they fashioned a wreath of myrtle, arborvitae, and flowers encircling a picture of two hands joined together with the motto, "What God has joined together let no man put asunder." A beautiful transparency was hung near the door of the church. Before 8:00 p.m., the sanctuary filled with friends and relatives, many of whom had to bring their own chairs because the new church was yet to be furnished.

Henry Oliver Lindeblad, the congregation's new pastor, officiated at the marriage ceremony. There were four bridesmaids—Alma's friends Hilma Freed and Sophia Brodd, her next-door neighbor Minnie Kohler, and Carl's sister Annie. The four groomsmen were Alma's brother Ephraim, Carl's brother John, and friends Oscar Landell and Eben Carlsson. A photo of the bridal couple shows that the groom was dressed in full suit, white tie, white gloves. The bride wore a long dress of white satin and tulle, tightly fitted at the waist, the skirt in a cascade of ruffles. A crown of myrtle held her floor length veil in place, and she wore elbow-length gloves. At her

Dr. and Mrs. Carl Swensson on their wedding day.

throat was a broach, perhaps a gift from her husband. Alma was almost twenty-one years old, and appears regal, confident, competent, capable.

Following the ceremony, more than two hundred guests walked with the couple to the bride's parents' home for a reception. There were beautiful gifts—a china set, a silver butter dish, a dozen silver spoons from Alma's high school classmates, a Swedish painting, a cake basket, napkin rings, a flower vase, a silver fruit dish and syrup pitcher, a card receiver from five young ladies of the church choir.[49] Carl and Alma would make good use of all their gifts at the parsonage in Lindsborg.

The members of the Swedish Evangelical Lutheran Church at Moline had watched Alma grow and mature into a gifted musician and warm friend. She was "one of their own." A handwritten poem, from the entire congregation, expressed their congratulations to Carl and Alma on their wedding day and their hopes for the future of the young couple:

To Pastor Carl A. Swensson and Miss Alma C. Lind
on their Wedding Day, the 15th of September, 1880

A wave on the Sea of Life
Brought you together and hand in hand
You have sworn to faithfully proceed
To the final goal of the unseen shore
That God has planned for you.
See above his words forever more.

Your promise dear will be easy kept
With steadfast love in your married life
Then nothing will impair
Your happiness from day to day
The road so hard to walk alone
Shall be easy for the two of you.
May gladness, health, peace, and happiness
Follow you throughout your lives
May your hearts be free of grief
May your love be crowned with bliss
This is our wish and prayer.

May your lives flow quietly
Like a calm stream among the flowers
And the lovely flowers tied into a wreath
Around your tender holy union
May the angels of peace guard your home.

For especially you, Mrs. Svensson, we send
Our heartfelt thanks and wishes warm and dear
May you feel the love of Jesus
Protecting you against the storms of life
And may you in your lovely home
Live in peace with the one you love.

Oh, how we miss you in our temple
No more we hear your lovely voice
And the temple singing that you led

But you shall always be remembered
It hurts to cut our fellowship with you
As we take your hand to say goodbye.

May we meet at last in eternal peace
When we have ceased to strive on earth
With God we'll light the wedding candle
In heaven with its perfect song
We wish to meet you there
In everlasting bliss.[50]

Surely Pastor Olof Olsson was among the guests at the marriage ceremony and reception. As he watched all of the people extend their best wishes to bride and groom on their wedding day, Olof may have thought to himself, "Carl and Alma—they are the best and the brightest."

Their future was ahead in the great American West, in Kansas.

A Partnership

Perhaps it was one of those autumn days when the sky was clearest and brightest blue. Like a long, cold drink of apple cider, one could marvel at the clarity of the prairie. Or perhaps it was one of those hot, dusty, dry autumn days when the incessant wind blows dust and prairie soil, and tumbleweeds roll down Main Street collecting in every available corner, and the cicadas drone on and on and on.

Whatever the weather was the day that Alma Christina Lind Swensson stepped off the train at the Lindsborg Depot with Carl in the early autumn of 1880, she entered a landscape that looked like no other place her twenty-one-year-old eyes had seen. No winding blue Mississippi River here like she had known in Moline. No birch trees. No trees at all, except for a few cottonwoods along the meandering Smoky Hill River, named for its dark, dusky water. But Carl could promise Alma that Kansas would provide sunsets of breath-taking color, and the moon glowing in the night sky would feel so close she could almost pluck it from the heavens.

In the village of Lindsborg there were a few clapboard stores sitting in the buffalo grass. One mud street defined east and west. The population was listed at 469, 194 of whom listed Sweden as their birth place. Most of the others were their children or grandchildren.

Farmers outside the village planted wheat and corn and broomcorn. Some people still lived in dugouts in the Lindsborg of 1880, even if they were somewhat temporary. Some people lived in stone houses, made of the ochre limestone quarried in nearby bluffs.[51]

If the landscape was foreign to her eyes, the people in the community may have seemed like long-lost cousins from Sweden. They spoke the same language; they shared a very similar cultural background and Lutheran faith. Early in her life, Alma, too, had experienced pioneer living.

Main Street, Lindsborg, Kansas, 1878.

Alma must have been encouraged to know that a world of opportunities awaited them both in this frontier village and farming region. She would be challenged to create a place of culture by using her musical skills and accomplishments to help lift people above their difficult, everyday existence. After all, a choir had already been planted by Olof Olsson from the very first worship service in that church of sod and stone a decade earlier.

From the moment she arrived in town, Alma was appointed organist at Bethany Lutheran Church. From the organ, she was a full partner in setting the atmosphere for worship. Alma also conducted the choir, and later she would conduct a brass ensemble to enhance congregational singing. Weddings, funerals, festive worship services—all these were before her.

Carl and Alma were both bright, strong, eager, enthusiastic, and their energy could hardly be contained. Already known for his inspiring oratory, Carl attacked his work with a ferocity that was breathtaking. Alma had the ability to help make the vision reality—step-by-step-by-step with quiet encouragement, intellect, and support, yet with her own genius for organization, hospitality, and leadership.

Lindsborg would be a vibrant community, a cultural oasis in the American West during the same era when Wyatt Earp and Bat Masterson were keeping law and order in Dodge City, Buffalo Bill was organizing his Wild West Show, and Phoebe Ann Mosey had yet to change her name to Annie Oakley but had already impressed Frank Butler with her expert marksmanship.

The Swenssons both knew that education was important. It would prepare those children of hardworking, immigrant farmers and shopkeepers, so use to the prairie's dusty streets, for America's limitless opportunities. They envisioned a school in Lindsborg that would provide both sound education and culture for the children who grew up in this small place.

Carl stated that the community's children "should obtain the necessary Christian education . . . among our youth, how many gifts that would otherwise be hidden and rust."[52] A school, the Swenssons thought, would help benefit and gladden the community and the church of God.

Unlike many schools of the era, this school would be coeducational from the beginning. Alma, whose growing-up years in Moline coincided with the blossoming of the women's suffrage and temperance movements, and whose parents insisted that she further her education, likely influenced Carl's thinking on this important subject. There were critics, but Carl had an answer for them: "As long as the good God allows boys and girls to be born into the same family together I do not know why I should not allow them to go to school together."[53] At Bethany, girls and boys both could dream great dreams and grow intellectually and spiritually.

Like their contemporary, author Hamlin Garland who would win the Pulitzer Prize in 1922,[54] Alma and Carl believed they need not look east to imitate literature, art, and music to enhance their community. They would define their place right exactly where they were on the Great Plains, near the center of the continental United States. The school would be an expression of the people of this prairie place. Instead of attracting elite teachers from the East Coast for their school, these sons and daughters of immigrant families would be taught by the best teachers Carl could recruit. They would know Swedish, and would study the high art and culture of the old homeland of the Lindsborg settlers. They would be graduates of educational institutions that had flourished since the Middle Ages. Joining the faculty within the decade would be Birger Sandzén from Skara and Lund universities and the Swedish Royal Academy; Hagbard Brasé and Oscar Thorsén, musicians who had studied at the Swedish Royal Conservatory; Carl Gustafson Lotave, who studied at the Swedish Artist's League; and Olaf Gräfstrom from the Royal Academy of Fine Arts, who was already so well known that the king of Sweden owned one of his paintings.

And the school, Carl and Alma hoped, would send their students east—to Yale for example, where the students from Lindsborg would demonstrate the values they learned growing up with sensibilities and responsibilities, the skills of surviving the hardships of blizzards and prairie fires, grasshoppers, and tornadoes, and the ability to live peaceably together in the close quarters of a dugout or sod house.

Carl, Alma, and the Bethany congregation made plans that were announced throughout the Smoky Valley. The sacristy of Bethany Lutheran Church would become a classroom during the week, much like European schools of learning. J. A. Udden, a brilliant, inquisitive, energetic new graduate of Augustana College, born in 1859 in Västergötland, was hired to be the first instructor. In a few years, he would become a renowned geologist with the publication of his research done at the Paint Creek Indian burial mounds just southwest of Lindsborg. Later in his career, he would help discover the Texas oil fields.

The date for the opening of school was set: October 15, 1881. With anticipation, Swensson and Udden waited in the sacristy that morning for pupils to arrive. And into the sacristy walked six boys and four girls to begin their education—John Johnson, Eric Olsson, Fredrik Carlson, Nora Lind,[55] Otto E. Håkanson, Andrew Cedarholm, Oscar Hobbart, Lovisa Olson, Johanna Fälling, and Jenny Carlson. Udden would teach classes of arithmetic, geography, English reading, Swedish reading, penmanship, orthography. Carl taught Bible and religious history.[56] Alma would see to it that the children who attended this new school would know music—such music that would last throughout their lives and on to their descendants, from one generation to another. It would be inspiring, noble, joyful music such that every generation would have the melody as a soundtrack all of their lives.

T. D. Wickersham, a plasterer who worked at Bethany Church in 1881 noted that Mrs. Swensson "is a practical musician and her vocal powers, to say the least, are splendid. She teaches the children of her husband's congregation music. She is a splendid teacher. Her pupils can run up and down the reel with great precision. This young couple, the pastor and wife, have started under very favorable surroundings in the battle of life and it is believed and hoped they will pull together for the shore."[57]

Alma likely helped her young students learn music for *Julotta*, 1881. Pastor Olof Olsson would be in town to visit members of his former congregation and take part in the service. An article in the December 29 issue of the *Lindsborg Localist*, "Christmas at Bethany Church," described *Julotta* that year, which began at 5:00 a.m. and concluded at 9:00 a.m. The author mentioned that both Pastor Swensson and Professor Olsson gave sermons that early Christmas morning, but the reporter was at a disadvantage because "our Swedish education has been sadly neglected." The reporter continued,

> As for the musical part, we could judge somewhat as to the merits of that, and must say it was equal to if not superior to anything we ever heard. The choir especially, showed superior ability and careful, intelligent training. The Bethany Church can congratulate themselves on having, in Mrs. Swensson, a lady of rare gifts and culture.[58]

As Carl was occupied with the school and his work as pastor of Bethany Church, Alma, in addition to the work of organist, choir director, and music teacher, made the parsonage their home—one of the largest homes in the village, where visitors would be warmly welcomed.

The academic preparation for students was high. By 1892, Uppsala and Lund universities in Sweden recognized students with degrees from Bethany College by permitting the recipients to enroll without taking entrance exams.[59] In 1893, Bethany graduates could enroll in the graduate schools of Yale and Chicago universities without any further studies or examinations. Between 1898 and 1902, twenty-one Bethany graduates enrolled at Yale. Seven of the twelve graduates of the class of 1899 studied at Yale. In 1902, Yale reported that the Bethany College Club of Yale "is a very vigorous and active organization. There are now more graduates from Bethany College in the Yale graduate school than from any other college, Yale excepted."[60]

The Messiah Festival

We understand that Rev. Swensson and lady and Mr. Hasselquist[61] of this city are busily engaged in working up a "Messiah" choir to comprise 100 voices. $50 has already been raised for song books. A leader for the choir and a string orchestra will be engaged from Rock Island. This choir is to give concerts during Easter at the different churches in this vicinity for the benefit of the Swedish Academy at Lindsborg (*Smoky Valley News*, December 8, 1881).

The Messiah Chorus was organized last Sunday with a membership of 38 from Lindsborg. The choir is to contain 100 voices, and the rest of the choir will be made up from Freemount, Assaria, and Salemsborg churches (*Smoky Valley News*, December 15, 1881).

The singers came to the parsonage first, warmly welcomed by Carl and Alma. They would learn some new music—something more difficult than they had ever tried before, but their pastor and his wife, who was their choir director and organist, believed they could do it. Prayers began the gathering along with words of encouragement. Perhaps there were scales to be sung to determine which voices were appropriate for which part. Alma handed out the new music. Carefully, the scores were opened. Carefully, the scores were read. The singing began—Handel's *Messiah*.

Handel's great oratorio came to Lindsborg via Moline and London, thanks to Pastor Olof Olsson, now a professor of theology at Augustana College and Seminary. On April 4, 1879, Olsson purchased a ticket while in London to attend a performance of *Messiah* at Exeter Hall led by the Italian born conductor and composer Sir Michael Costa. Olsson's ticket was high in the balcony, but with a direct view of the 600-member chorus and orchestra. The gentleman sitting next to Olsson shared with him a copy of the score. Handel's music made Olsson's heart and spirit soar. "At times I was so carried away that I was hardly aware of myself," Olsson later wrote. When the chorus and orchestra came to the "Hallelujah Chorus," Olsson said ". . . I was so thrilled through bone and marrow that I feared the shock would be too great for me."[62] When he returned to Augustana in the spring of 1880, Olsson brought together friends and acquaintances to learn the oratorio, and soon a choir was meeting several times a week. One can easily presume that Olsson asked the gifted, talented organist Alma Lind to help organize the singers and assist with rehearsals. This is likely how Alma learned Handel's masterpiece.

Augustana's Handel Society presented *Messiah* for the first time on April 11, 1881. Later that spring, the chorus sang again at First Congregational Church in Moline as part of the commencement festivities for the college. Carl Aaron Swensson was in the audience for that performance, and surely Alma sat beside him. She certainly would have traveled to Moline with Carl for the opportunity to visit her family and hear the concert that she had a hand in organizing.

Now Alma taught Handel's music to the Lindsborg singers note by note, line by line, phrase by phrase. Along with teaching the music came teaching the annunciation and pronunciation of the text. This was no easy task, for the language the singers spoke in their daily lives was Swedish—the language of commerce, industry, farming, home making, pharmacy, at the grocery store, with the undertaker, at the blacksmith, in the post office, at the livery, with the dressmaker and milliner, at the bank, at the flour mill, in the brick yard, at the insurance company, at the creamery, and of the church. But Handel's great oratorio would be sung in English.

Alma Swensson pushed for excellence—with patience. All winter long—from December of 1881 and January and February and into March of 1882—the singers came twice each week on sleighs or lumber wagons across the fields or on foot to rehearse seven choruses of the oratorio:

And the Glory of the Lord
O Thou That Tellest Good Tidings to Zion
Behold the Lamb of God
All We Like Sheep Have Gone Astray

Lift Up Your Heads
Hallelujah!
Worthy Is the Lamb, Amen

It was an ambitious project—perhaps more than anyone, even Alma herself, had imagined. But her people were willing to work! Reports have come down through the years that people were eager to learn. Singing such a masterpiece was something greater than themselves. The tedium, the loneliness, and the worries of day-to-day existence could be forgotten for a while as people became a choir—a collaborative, a collective, striving to make something beautiful for the glory of God and an accomplishment for themselves. Alma did more than her part as music conductor, organist, and teacher. She brought them together in community.

Lindsborg historian Dr. Emory Lindquist writes,

> The *Messiah* was to be identified with the daily life of the people. It was to become a part of them, an expression of their love for the beautiful. They came from simply furnished sod-houses, stone houses, and frame houses to sing the *Messiah*. For some of them, it involved a rough ride over roads filled with ruts as the lumber-wagon bounced them here and there. Still others walked miles across the prairies to the stone church which meant so much to them. Neighbor joined neighbor, and as they rode under the clear, starlit, Kansas sky, they intoned a chorus from *Messiah*. It made life meaningful as they shared in this great venture of cooperation.[63]

At rehearsals and later on the stage, all were equal—setting aside their daily role as farmer, physician, shopkeeper, custodian, teacher, homemaker.

As the earth turned toward spring, rehearsals continued, twice each week. Alma organized sectional rehearsals that were held both in the church and in the parsonage. These were three intense months of choral singing. The first presentation would be given March 28. Arrangements were made to bring to Lindsborg the Augustana College orchestra under the direction of Joseph Osborn, who had conducted *Messiah* in Rock Island. The organist would be none other than Dr. Olof Olsson himself. With the experienced musicians in place, Alma would be one of the soprano soloists. The others were Lydia Andreen, soprano; Anna Swensson, alto; C. A. Backman, tenor; F. Linder, bass.[64]

The audience assembled at Bethany Church on that Sunday evening, March 28, 1882. Programs were printed in Swedish and English. The chorus filed in to the front of the sanctuary—women and men both wearing black. At 7:30 the orchestra from Augustana College began the gentle "Overture/ Pastoral Symphony." The tenor, C. A. Backman stood in place and began the broad recitative, "Comfort ye . . . " At that moment, the Kansas people began what would become their great annual presentation of Handel's *Messiah*—a tradition continuing for more than 130 years. The soprano solos were "How Beautiful Are the Feet of Those Who Preach the Gospel of Peace" and "I Know that My Redeemer Liveth."

The next day, March 29, the chorus and orchestra travelled in lumber wagons north over the fields to Salemsborg Lutheran Church. On March 30, the *Lindsborg Localist* carried a review by its editor:

> After thorough preparation, the Bethania Chorus, numbering some seventy-five on the evening of the 28th. The church was filled with a fine audience who enjoyed a rare musical treat. It has always been held that to render the *Messiah* is a most difficult and delicate undertaking, which to accomplish is glory enough for any company of singers. Therefore, anything like success by amateurs is no small praise. The performance on the whole, was good, while some of it was excellent, especially the Hallelujah Chorus and the solos by Mrs. Alma Swensson, Soprano, and Miss Anna Swensson, Alto.

The singers must have been delighted to read the paper as they traveled on the Union Pacific to the Salina Opera House on March 30 for the third presentation. Then, on March 31, the Union Pacific took the singers and orchestra to the McPherson Opera House; three days later, lumber wagons headed once again over the fields, this time west to the Fremont Lutheran Church for the last presentation of the year.

From the telescope of the twenty-first century, looking backward in time, one cannot help but think of the sense of accomplishment the singers and their young director must have felt. Alma launched a sense of confidence in them all—in what they, here on the broad Great Plains, could do themselves. She came to know the members of her choir in that intimate sort of way when people become one ensemble for the purpose of making music. She helped lift their vision of what they could do together.

Years later, on the eve of the fortieth anniversary of that first performance, Alma Christina Lind Swensson would disclaim any credit for the achievements. To a reporter for *The New York Times*, she said that it is the Christian faith of the people of Lindsborg which inspires them to sing. "The chorus is an expression of the faith of my people," she told the reporter. "Without inspiration from God, it would fail."

On August 21, 1882, Alma gave birth to their first child, Bertha Maria Fredrika—Maria for her father's mother, Maria Blixt Swensson who died when Carl was seventeen years old, and Fredrika for Alma's mother, who lived in Moline. On February 11, 1885, Annie (always pronounced "ahnnie") Hilma Theodora was born. The family was complete. The four Swenssons became devoted to each other as well as to the vision Carl and Alma held for the church and the community.

Where Hospitality Is Golden

Alma and Carl, Bertha and Annie lived in the parsonage of Bethany Lutheran Church. It was one of the largest houses in Lindsborg, the place that would host guests and events that became benchmarks in the life and times of the college, church, and community.

By 1889, Carl was not only pastor of the Bethany congregation, now numbering nearly a thousand members, but he was also president of Bethany College.[65]

Carl recruited new professors to increase the educational offerings and new business people to the community to broaden the services offered in Lindsborg—a town with growing name recognition, thanks to Carl's increasing stature among Swedish Americans, as well as the Messiah Festival, whose renown grew each year. When the "new recruits" came to town, Alma provided a warm and gracious introduction to the community.

Carl recruited a photographer to Lindsborg—a young husband and wife team who had already established a studio in Round Rock, Texas. Like almost every one of his recruits, Bror and Sarah Noyd Gröndal were born in Sweden. The story about the Gröndals goes something like this: "Say," Swensson told Bror and Sarah when he visited them during an 1887 church gathering in Round Rock, "our little place could use a good photographer." As the conversation progressed, Swensson was so convincing of the merits and wonders of Lindsborg and Kansas and Bethany College that the Gröndals moved their studio to Lindsborg's Main Street. For more than sixty years the Gröndal Studio captured the life and times and landscape of college and community through his photographs.[66] Sarah Noyd and Alma were the same age and discovered they had lived in Andover at the same time.

King Oscar II of Sweden already owned a painting by Olof Gräfstrom, whom Carl recruited to Bethany College in 1893 to establish the fine art department. Gräfstrom had studied at the Royal Academy of Fine Arts in Stockholm with Anders Zorn, Richard Berg, and Bruno Liljefors.

A young Birger Sandzén, home in Sweden from a year of art and voice lessons in Paris, wrote a detailed letter to Carl Swensson in 1894 "respectfully seeking a position in the service of your college, just for a year or two." At the Swedish universities of Skara and Lund, Sandzén studied French, literature, and aesthetics, then moved to Stockholm where he became one of eight pupils in Zorn's private studio. Carl answered Sandzén's letter in the affirmative, and Sandzén came to teach painting and drawing, French and voice. He stayed not for "a year or two", but for sixty-one years! His first temporary home in Lindsborg was with Carl and Alma at the parsonage.

G. N. Malm, who came to Lindsborg in 1894, achieved national renown as a businessman, interior designer, artist, journalist, and author. Born in Sweden, Malm finished *Jönköpong allmäna läaroverk* at the age of fourteen, then was apprenticed to the master painter Jonas Lindqvist and learned the craft of decoration. He followed his parents to Nebraska where he wrote for Swedish-American newspapers. Carl Swensson met him during a business trip to Omaha, and they engaged in a long conversation where Carl is reported to have said, "Omaha is not the place for you. We need you in Lindsborg." Soon G. N. Malm and his young wife, Mathilda, moved to Lindsborg where Swensson put him to work on the interior design of the chapel, classrooms, and offices of the college's newly constructed Main Building.[67]

Carl Gustafson Lotave, a student of the Artists League in Stockholm, came to Lindsborg from Lidköping, Sweden, and assumed the art position when Gräfstrom accepted a teaching post at Augustana College, Rock Island.

Hagbard Brasé came to Bethany College in 1900 to be professor of harmony and composition and the college organist. He had just completed his studies at Skara University and the Royal Conservatory of Music in Stockholm. Brasé soon was named conductor of the Bethany Oratorio Society, a position he held for more than forty years. Oscar Thorsen, a native of Västergötland and graduate of Skara, joined the faculty in 1901 as a piano instructor.

To these new faculty members, Alma offered an open door, a warm handshake, and often meals and a bed for their first few nights on the

Kansas prairie. She shared with them the early vision of making this a college for young people seeking the American dream. Sandzén observed that "there was beautiful Christian fellowship in the Swensson home. Mrs. Swensson was a good wife, mother, and hostess. Her clear and practical understanding and her good judgment were often an invaluable help to her sanguine husband. Her abilities, patience, and hospitality were often tested, we may be sure of that. The benevolent and hos-

Carl, Bertha, Alma, and Annie Swensson

pitable Dr. Swensson often brought home unexpected guests to dinner or supper, such as students with their parents, farmers, fellow clergymen, and strangers whom he met in town or in his college office." Sandzén noted that he witnessed some of these surprises himself, "and I will testify that Mrs. Swensson was always able to make the best of the situation with cheerfulness and cordiality. A visit in the parsonage was an unforgettable pleasure, whether one was invited or not."[68]

And many guests were invited to the parsonage. The Swenssons entertained on behalf of church, college, and community, such as T. N. Hasselquist, the president of the Augustana Synod; Pastor Erland Carlsson, the immigrant pastor and Augustana Synod leader; Emmy Carlsson Evald, president of the Augustana Women's Missionary Society; Olof Olsson who came back to Lindsborg on several occasions; the well-known Chicago architect L. G. Hallberg, who brought plans for the Main Building constructed during 1885 and 1886; Colonel C. F. Smith, a lumberman from St. Paul, Minnesota who made possible the building of Ling Auditorium in 1894—an unusual hexagonal pavilion of wood where *Messiah* would be presented each year. Smith became a major philanthropist to Bethany College.

Senators, governors, commissioners, ambassadors, and bishops came to the parsonage for conversation, theological discussion, and Alma's hospitality.

Generations of early Bethany College students often recalled the final event of their graduation ceremonies—an invitation from Carl and Alma to the parsonage to be together one last time. Under the Kansas summer sky, the new graduates enjoyed refreshments, and then would sing together in four part harmony, "Nearer My God to Thee," which became the unofficial Bethany hymn, one of Carl's favorites.[69]

Alma hosted one of the most significant events in the history of the Augustana Synod. On June 6, 1892, during the meeting of the Synod at Lindsborg, fifty women from all over the country were present on the lawn of the parsonage when the decision was made to organize a women's missionary society. The women, wives of pastors and lay delegates, came to the parsonage expecting a typical, bountiful Swedish coffee party. But Alma and Emmy Evald had an additional purpose in mind. Emmy gave a powerful speech about the need to organize themselves for the work of the church around the world. She based her speech on the message Jesus gave Mary and Mary Magdalene in Matthew 28: "Go quickly and tell." Emmy and Alma asked the ladies to sign a document requesting permission from the synod to organize a women's missionary society. The fifty women agreed. Then, carrying banners with red crosses, they formed a procession to bring their request to the business meeting of the synod in session at Bethany Church. The delegates, all male, had a heated debate for several hours.[70] Carl Swensson spoke in favor of the organization as did Emmy's husband, Pastor Carl Evald. The request passed, the women returned to the parsonage for prayer and thanksgiving, and elected officers. Emmy Evald was elected president and Alma recording secretary. The Augustana Women's Missionary Society came into existence that day at Alma's house, empowering women in the church for social ministry and action as well as experience in leadership. Now women would serve on congregational Women's Missionary Society boards of directors, conduct meetings, draft by-laws, organize events, and learn to raise money in support of missionaries, hospitals, and schools.[71]

Alma Lind Swensson would become a prominent figure in the work of this organization, and she would bring a world view to thousands of women across the United States.

In the Presence of Kings and Queens

When she was thirty-seven years old, in the summer of 1897, Alma Swensson accompanied Carl on a voyage to Sweden. On their way, they would visit London, Paris, and Berlin. They would attend ceremonies at the General Art and Industrial Exhibition of Stockholm, a diocesan meeting in Härnosand, and a reception honoring King Oscar II during his jubilee. There were others from Bethany College in their party—Professors Laurin, Thorstenberg, Floren, and Sandzén. The Swensson daughters, Bertha, age fifteen, and Annie, age thirteen, would stay home with their aunts, uncles, and friends.

Alma had much to get ready. An organist had to be secured for the two months while Alma would be away from Bethany Church. As recording secretary of the Augustana Women's Missionary Society, she had to make sure those responsibilities were covered as well. Perhaps there were gifts to take to the people they would visit along the way—gifts from Bethany Church, Bethany College, and Lindsborg. And of course there were decisions to be made regarding clothing for the journey. Summer in Sweden would be quite different than summer in Kansas. Did she have the appropriate clothes to wear to the receptions, banquets, meetings, services, tours? What would she need for an ocean voyage?

The Lindsborg party took the Missouri Pacific to Kansas City where they boarded the Santa Fe to Chicago. From Chicago they took the Grand Trunk which brought them through Canada to Niagara Falls and finally to New York City. The highlight of their day in New York was a visit to the tomb of Ulysses S. Grant, which had just been dedicated on April 27. "It was an hour of worship, of devotion, and healthful meditation," Carl wrote. At Battery Park they stopped at the monument to John Ericsson, the distinguished Swedish-American inventor and engineer who developed the ironclad ship the *USS Monitor*, which was so instrumental in the Civil War. They would also visit Ericsson's tomb in Sweden.[72]

The party left New York harbor on Friday, May 28 on board the *S.S. Mongolian*. Carl wrote of four people with whom he discussed world events: The Anglican bishop, Rev. Gray of Florida; Dr. Lawson of Brooklyn; Mr. Mau of Ceylon, Mexico, and England; and the six-foot-three Major J. B. Pond of New York who had visited Kansas in 1858. There were shipboard lectures, one by Carl himself where he extolled Swedes, Swedish-Americans, Lutherans, Bethany College, and life on the great American prairie. Professors Laurin and Thorstenberg provided piano concerts. Carl noted that members of his party sang several numbers. Perhaps Alma favored them all with a solo.

On June 9, the *S.S. Mongolian* stopped at Meville, Ireland, and the next day sailed up the Clyde to Glasgow and then into London. The city was bustling with thousands and thousands of people from all over the globe to celebrate the seventy-five-year reign of Queen Victoria.

On Monday, June 14, Thorstenberg, Sandzén, Floren, Laurin, Carl, and Alma were in the audience for the triennial Handel Festival at the Crystal Palace. A chorus and orchestra of 3,500 performers were led by conductor August Manns and sang *Messiah*. The soloists were Madame Albani, Miss Ella Russell, Madame Clara Samuell, and Madame Nordica, who in 1902 would sing at Lindsborg's own Messiah Festival.

One might wonder what the Lindsborg people thought as they sat listening to the presentation. They knew the score well—Alma and Thorstenberg had conducted the oratorio, Sandzén had sung the tenor solos, and Alma the soprano solos. Carl was likely comparing the size of the crowd to those that attended the performance at home. Perhaps Alma had thoughts on how the voices blended and the articulation of the British singers. Thorstenberg might have noted the tempo of the music and the balance between orchestra and chorus.

On another day in London, the group visited the treasures of the British Museum, the houses of Parliament, and Poets Corner in Westminster Abbey where they stood before a white marble medallion honoring the beloved Swedish Nightingale, Jenny Lind. They noted the inscription: "I know that my Redeemer liveth," the aria from *Messiah* that she had made famous in her repertoire.

While in Paris, Sandzén, who studied art and music there in 1894, acted as interpreter and tour guide for the Lindsborg travelers.[73] They saw the wonders of the Louvre and the soaring heights of Notre Dame.[74]

A train to Germany brought them to the Cologne Cathedral where they gazed at the gold sarcophagus that legend says holds the relics of the Three Wisemen, brought from Milan by Rainald von Dassel in 1124. Outside the cathedral they were suddenly caught up in a throng of people watching a military parade in honor of Kaiser Wilhelm II.

What a feast this must have been for Alma—a feast for her eyes and for her spirit—the great museums, the great world capitals steeped in history, the archaeology of old cities, the music of symphony orchestras, the art of the masters. And Sweden was still ahead.

Laurin and Sandzén looked forward to being home in Sweden, the country they had left within the decade to teach in Kansas. Alma may have had faint memories from her childhood; she was returning to Sweden for the first time since she left with her parents and brother in 1864. Thorstenberg and Carl were born and raised in America. But Carl was the epitome of Sweden in the United States, and this was his second visit to the ancestral homeland.

When the Lindsborg folks reached Malmö, the port city on Sweden's southern coast of Skåne, they boarded a train to Stockholm. Here they visited an exhibit of Scandinavia's most famous painters of the day—works by Anders Zorn and Richard Berg with whom Sandzén had studied before coming to Lindsborg; Carl Larssson who depicted Swedish home life created by his wife Karin in the village of Sundborn; Bruno Liljefors; Evan Bonnier; Elizabeth Keyser; and Prins Eugen himself, the king's son and a Renaissance man. Norwegian artists exhibiting their paintings included Erik Werenskjold, Otto Sinding, and Eilif Petersen. And from the art colony at Skagen, Denmark—just at the point where the Skagerrak and Kattegat come together—the artists Krøger, Viggo, Paulson, and Ancher brought their impressions of fisherfolk, farmers, and families. The quintet of people from Lindsborg, Kansas, mingled with the artists and visitors from around the world.

The Kansas travelers would return to Stockholm, but first they were scheduled to attend a meeting of the diocese at Härnösand. They traveled by carriage, steamer, buggy, rowboat, and lumber barge, across lakes, down rivers, and through fjords. It was June—the most glorious month in Sweden. Wildflowers—*blåklint, pröstkraje, lin, ängsklocka, smörblomma, blåklocka, vresros, vildkaprifol*—profusely lined their roadways. The mornings were sparkling with sun and cool air. The Nordic light continued long into the evenings as a backdrop for outdoor gatherings and evening refreshment.

Carl had the honor of preaching at Härnösand's Cathedral during the diocesan conference. At a grand dinner afterward, Alma was seated to the left of the Archbishop. Toasts were made to Carl Swensson. Then Carl raised his glass and responded by toasting the Swedish Lutheran women—"our mothers and wives, our sisters, our daughters." This may have been Carl's way of paying tribute in a very public way to his own wife and what she meant to his life and his mission. He was clearly proud of his wife and simply in love with her.[75]

Another day, the Swenssons and the bishop made a call at Fridhem, the summer residence of Prince Bernadotte on the island of Visby. Here they offered greetings from Lindsborg to Princess Ebbe Bernadotte and the royal children.

In Norrland, Carl and Alma encountered the King of Siam, Chulalongkorn, also in Sweden to celebrate the jubilee. Chulalongkorn caused a delay in the Swensson's travel itinerary when the entire steamer line was taken by the king and his entourage.

Another leg of their travels found them on the lumber steamer *Verandi* as they sailed through Gafviksfjärden. Carl wrote

> The water is calm and its surface forms a great, shining mirror. Look at that mountain to the left, that long continuation of hills, to the right, another mountain further on, seen in a paler light. Notice the many inlets, islands and terraces. It has rained a little. See the indescribable veil of the light, airy mist, cast over parts of the view, not hiding, but rather calling attention to its beauties. I shall never forget the charms of that hour.[76]

The ship was met by the pastor of Nordingrå and his two hired men. Carl and Alma climbed on a low flatboat with settees for the passengers. The young hired men rowed the boat a mile to Nordingrå where the pastor's wife greeted them. She is "hospitable, kind-hearted and intelligent," Carl wrote,[77] and they walked up the hill to the parsonage. Dinner was waiting—a veritable Swedish *smörgåsbord* with delectable offerings of fried perch and another kind of fish, omelettes with mushrooms, veal-cutlets and potatoes, strawberries and cream, tea, chocolate, Swedish beer. And afterward, they took a long walk under the *Midsommar* night sky.

Carl and Alma made a trip to the heart of Sweden—to Dalecarlia and, with Sandzén, visited the great artist Zorn at his studio in Mora and his newly completed home, Zorngården. Zorn, who had received the Legion of Honor at the 1889 world exhibition in Paris, already had captured America's imagination with his presence at the 1893 Chicago World's Fair. During his stay in America, he was commissioned to paint portraits of businessmen, grande dames of society—including Bertha Honore Palmer—portraits of presidents Grover Cleveland and William Howard Taft, an etching of Theodore Roosevelt that later became a painting, and a portrait of First Lady Frances Folsom Cleveland. Sandzén had studied many hours in Zorn's atelier in Stockholm and considered him his most influential teacher.

A very personal journey took them to Unnaryd where Carl visited the home of his mother, Maria Blixt. There they met an old couple who had heard his father, Jonas Swensson, preach more than forty years earlier. Carl's aunt, still living, provided a kind "welcome home" to her American nephew who was just seventeen when his mother died.

Back in Stockholm, the Swenssons visited the Royal Palace and Riddarholm Church, the burial place of Sweden's kings and queens. They took a steamship to Gripsholm, the royal castle at Mariefred, and then walked the streets of Skansen, the open air museum established six years earlier.

In early August, Alma and Carl arrived in Uppsala where he would preach in the cathedral—the seat of the archbishop of Sweden, and the largest cathedral in all of Scandinavia. The eloquence of the building, the setting of the landmark, and the symbolism of the ancient house of worship made a marked impression on the Swedish-Americans from Kansas. The cathedral's magnificent twin spires rose 390 feet in the air. Consecrated in 1435, it became a pilgrim's church where people paid homage at Saint Eric's shrine. Inside the cathedral, sunlight streamed through stained glass windows, illuminating wall and ceiling paintings over and along the nave, which stretched 390 feet before them. The pulpit, where Carl would preach, was of gold leaf, a gift from the Queen Dowager Hedvig Eleonora. Designed by the Swedish baroque architect Nikodemus Tessin, it was sculpted by the cabinet-maker Burchard Precht in the style of 1710.

On Sunday morning, August 8, Alma was seated in Uppsala Cathedral under the nave that arched eighty-nine feet above the congregation. Here was the root of her faith, her home, and the language that spoke to her heart. She watched Carl process with the other clergy into the sanctuary to the music of the magnificent cathedral organ. The organist modulated to the appropriate key. There was a pause. Then the presiding pastor intoned, "*Helig, Helig, Helig är Herren Sebaot. Hela jorden är full av hans härlighet.*" With the congregation, she began singing the Lutheran liturgy which she knew in the fiber of her being. After Confession of Sins, the Kyrie, the Gloria, the Salutation, and the Collect, the Lessons and Gospel were read. The creeds were said, then an anthem was sung by the choir. Now Alma watched Carl climb into the ornate pulpit. He put his powerful hands beside the lectern, looked out across the congregation, and in his thirty-nine-year-old voice, from the heart of the heartland of America, delivered the sermon for the day. Alma listened to the voice she knew so well.

The visit to Sweden allowed Alma to observe a formal manner of entertaining, as she and Carl experienced a near-royal welcome. She noted the special touches made for important occasions. The concept of *smörgåsbord* gave sensibility to entertaining large groups of people. Her attentiveness would serve her well in four years when she and Carl would entertain distinguished visitors from Sweden and the United States to celebrate the jubilee of Bethany College.

Near the end of their journey to Sweden, Carl and Alma met King Oscar II at his summer home on Marstrand, on the southwest coast of Sweden. First they stopped at the residence of Bishop Johansson in Göteborg where they were overnight guests. The whole party climbed the rugged, rocky hills to take in the salty sea air, then they boarded a ship to Marstrand.

At 8:30 p.m., the Swenssons attended a soiree with the king as the honored guest. Carl reported that King Oscar was six-foot-three-inches tall, with a full, gray beard trimmed short, and though he was sixty-eight years old, "his gait is that of a young man!" Carl wrote. Carl and Alma had a brief, personal audience with the King whom, Carl said, "well remembered Bethany College." The king inquired of the Swenssons their impressions of his kingdom, especially the Stockholm exposition. The king remarked, "Here I live in peace and joy with my people." At the end of the evening, all the guests boarded a steamer to return to Göteborg. As the ship sailed away, King Oscar stood on the Marstrand shore and waved his goodbye.

Their journey now complete, the party made the voyage back to the United States and, via train, came home to Lindsborg where they were met at the depot by family members and closest friends who brought Carl and Alma to the college dining room. More than 500 people had assembled to welcome them home with cheers and applause.[78]

Home to Kansas

The wide, panoramic prairie of Kansas with breathtaking sunsets and horizontal grandeur became home to Carl and Alma's families, and Lindsborg is where they settled. The first issue of the Lindsborg *News* at the turn of the century to 1900 reported that Johan and Fredrika, Alma's parents, took up residence in Lindsborg, too. They had lived in Illinois since their emigration to America in 1864. Now, at the ages of eighty-six and sixty-six, they would be near their four children who had settled in the college town. Their oldest daughter Alma, of course, was comfortably settled in the parsonage. She was the organist and choir director at Bethany Church and first lady of both church and college. Their son, Herman, had lived in Lindsborg since 1886, and now owned a men's clothing store on Main Street. He later married Ella Peterson of the community. Anna Nora would marry George Eberhardt, a local banker and insurance broker. Jenny was the competent, efficient, and able secretary to the president of Bethany College, Carl. The Lind's oldest son, Ephraim, who was born in Sweden and immigrated with his parents and sister Alma, died in October 1881, in Iowa. A daughter, Hilma, died in Illinois in 1899. Their youngest child, Lars, is said to have run away from home.

Carl's brother, Luther Swensson, served as Lindsborg's postmaster and married Hannah M. Olson. Anna Maria Swensson married Eben Carlsson, who was the pharmacist. Eben was the son of the pioneer Swedish Lutheran pastor couple, Dr. Erland and Eva Charlotta Carlsson who, in their retirement, purchased a farm just northeast of Lindsborg and were frequent visitors at the Bethany parsonage. Eben's sister was Emmy Carlsson Evald, Alma's great friend and co-founder of the Augustana Women's Missionary Society. John Swensson's career took him to Jamestown, New York, where he and his wife, Marie, served as superintendent and matron of Gustavus Adolphus Children's Home.

Alma and Carl's home, the Bethany Church parsonage, became the gathering place for all the family. Through the rehearsal season of the oratorio society that spring of 1900, Alma, Jenny, Nora, and Herman helped their parents adjust to their new location. The family had been together for just a few months when Fredrika became ill, then died in March. The newspaper reported that loving hands decorated Bethany Church for the funeral and a double quartet sang "very pretty music." Dr. Floren of Salina preached the sermon. In his remarks, Dr. Pihlblad, assistant pastor of the church and vice president of the college, called Fredrika "a faithful, earnest Christian." She was the first of the family to be buried on the Kansas prairie, at Elmwood Cemetery.[79]

In April 1900, the *Ladies' Home Journal* carried an article by journalist Charles M. Harger, "Singing the *Messiah* on the Plains." The photogravure-style layout had photos of the chorus, the soloists, Carl Swensson and Samuel Thorstenberg, photos of the train depot with crowds of people arriving for the Messiah Festival, and of Ling Auditorium where *Messiah* was sung. The Swedes, Harger wrote, "are a singing people, and the religious sentiment is strong in their hearts." Harger describes the founding of the college and the oratorio society, the qualities of the people, a glowing review of the *Messiah* performance, and the affect upon its listeners:

> When the last note has died away, when the final Amen has been breathed, the listeners, their hearts warmed with religious fervor and exaltation, go out into the starry night as in a dream. The far horizon seems nearer, and the wide arch of heaven, bending over the dusky reaches of prairie sod and field closer at hand. . . . With such concentration of effort, such delight in musical expression, so worthy a theme, and so devout a people, little wonder is it that the singing of the Easter *Messiah* on the plains is an occasion to be anticipated eagerly, enjoyed with zest, and remembered long![80]

Soon after the oratorio society put their scores aside for the summer, the college, congregation, and community received word that their founder, Olof Olsson, now president of Augustana College and Seminary, had died after a long illness. Carl led the delegation from Lindsborg to Rock Island for the services held on May 16 at the chapel of Augustana College and at the Swedish Evangelical Lutheran Church in Moline, where Olsson and his family had been members for almost a quarter century. A long funeral procession brought Olsson's body to Riverside Cemetery, where he was buried next to his wife, Anna Lisa, who had died in 1887. Their graves are on a terrace, just below the top of the bluff, high above the Mississippi River.

Now speculation ran rampant throughout the synod about who would succeed Olsson as president of the college and seminary. The synod met in June 1900 at Burlington, Iowa, and Carl was handily elected to the position. He was the natural successor to Olsson—perhaps the one who knew more about education and the church's role in education than anyone else, for Carl was both president of a college and pastor of a church, nationally and internationally renowned. Alma, who attended the annual meeting of the Augustana Women's Missionary Society at the same time, must have considered how her life could change as the wife of the college and seminary president, and she may have thought that the change would be good for Carl's health. He could be more focused on the demands of one job without spreading himself so thin across church, college, conference leadership roles, newspaper writing, editing, and publishing. Alma would be near to her longtime friend Emmy Evald and the two of them could lead the Women's Missionary Society to greater service. It was an idea, a way of life, perhaps, that Alma may have secretly smiled about. Carl was honored by the election, but he asked the synod for time to think over the decision.

Carl and Alma came home to Lindsborg after the synod meeting and were met at the depot by a crowd of friends who brought them to Ling Auditorium where a full house had assembled. Speeches were made by Rev. Pilhlblad, Dr. Floren, and the Honorable Frank Grottan of McPherson. Carl was presented with a gift of $1,000. Whether the gift had any impact on his decision, and the course of discussion he had with Alma, will never be known, but Carl sent word to the synod. He would remain at Bethany. The announcement was made in the Lindsborg *News*, July 13, 1900.

After school started in the fall, Carl undertook an extensive lecture tour through Illinois, Iowa, Minnesota, Nebraska, and Kansas on behalf of the McKinley-Roosevelt presidential ticket. "We are so lonesome when the Dr. is away" the Lindsborg *News* stated, "and we hail his return with pleasure."

Whenever Carl was away, the home front continued as usual. Alma wrote him letters, often beginning, "My Dearest Carl. God's Peace." Occasionally she began her letters, "My kind little friend. God's Peace." Then she wrote of people who called at the parsonage:

> Pastor Seleen greets you, he stopped here for supper. . . . Mr. Falling came and invited us to dinner. . . . Mr. and Mrs. Hasselquist came and stayed a while in the evening. . . . Mrs. Olson is coming this afternoon. She came over this morning and was so worried about her husband's health that she cried, and so she stayed. Think so much about Mrs. Olson.[81]

> . . . four young men came to supper—Frank, Westerlund, Larson, and Renstrom. . . . Carlson came today.[82]

> . . . Norlunds brought fish yesterday evening. John Anderson, Hedlunds, and just now Johnson is here with some he has himself caught. I will try to save some until you come home, but then you must come as quickly as possible, do you hear?[83]

Alma missed Carl desperately when he was away.

> It is so empty after you left today and yesterday evening it was terribly dreary I couldn't sleep at night. Before I went to rest yesterday evening I thought how dependent I am on you and how empty it is when you are not near. . . . The week will surely be long. I hope you can come home as soon as you can.

> Many greetings and kisses from your most beloved Alma[84]

> This week has sure been long. If I could only be satisfied and grow accustomed to being alone—but that will never happen. It is just as difficult each time.

> Many greetings and kisses from the little ones and me!

> Your dearly devoted Alma[85]

Carl wrote letters while on the road, sharing the experiences of his journey, the weather, and sometimes the state of his health. His affection of her was apparent as he signed his letters,

God bless you, my dearest Alma. Lovingly, Carl[86]

A million kisses and hugs, Lovingly, Carl[87]

Love and greetings to you all. Three million kisses and embraces to you, Lovingly, Carl[88]

Carl returned from his political speaking tour of 1900 by November's election day, November 6.

The Lindsborg community gathered on election night at Ling Auditorium to listen to a concert by the Bethany Band. In between numbers, election results were read on stage, brought by a runner from the train depot where the results came in over the ticker tape. McKinley and Roosevelt carried all the states where Carl had been on a speaking tour and won the presidential election over William Jennings Bryon and Adlai Stevenson.

Soon after the election, Carl was being promoted in the Swedish-American press and regional newspapers to be appointed the new United States minister to Sweden and Norway.[89] It would have been a coup for the United States to have a couple—Carl and Alma—so associated with generations of Swedes in the heart of the heartland, where millions of Swedish people settled. Carl and Alma could speak with authentic voices on cultural, educational, economic, and agricultural issues. They knew the language. Such an appointment would require their move to Stockholm where they would live in the ambassador's residence with their daughters. There would be expectations of diplomatic entertaining, of course, and of being presented at court where Carl was already well known. They would travel throughout Sweden and Norway on behalf of the United States. Carl and Alma would have handled it beautifully, but it was not to be. W. W. Thomas, the current U.S. ambassador, was re-appointed, and he served through 1905.

The Jubilee Year—1901

It was the crowning year of their lives together—1901—the year that marked the twentieth anniversary of the founding of Bethany College, the thirty-second year since the first Swedish immigrants came to the Smoky Valley and founded Bethany Lutheran Church, and the twenty-first year of their marriage. Though they did not know it at the time, the events celebrating the twentieth anniversary of the college would mark their greatest achievement together, with the exception of their devoted, intelligent, beautiful, and talented daughters, Bertha and Annie.

The planning for the Jubilee celebration must have been more than a year in its organization. Perhaps they even discussed ideas on their trip through Sweden in 1897. The celebration was designed to mark the college's place, indeed the entire community's place, in the realm of education, the church, the world of music, politics, the connection with Sweden, and hospitality. The organization and execution of the events are staggering even to twenty-first century event planners.

The festivities were scheduled for November 9 through 12. The occasion was organized to recognize the role of Christian education in the church, showcase the brilliant young students of Bethany College, underscore the firm contemporary bonds between Lindsborg and Sweden, and highlight the achievements of this particular Swedish-American community. Invited guests would include politicians, professors, a host of pastors, church officials, and business leaders. The events would be open to the public—to the citizens of Lindsborg—and this more than anything, perhaps, put Carl and Alma's town firmly on the world stage.

Alma's gracious hospitality would warm the event. She and Carl would host distinguished visitors overnight in the new and larger Bethany Lutheran Church parsonage built by the Palmquist brothers and squarely facing Main Street with a broad front lawn. Their daughters, while helping with the entertaining and programs, perhaps gave up their rooms and stayed with relatives. The Brunswick Hotel would suffice for some visitors, but Alma asked if others would open their homes as well.

For her own home, Alma had to plan four days of breakfasts, midday meals, suppers, and coffee and refreshment in between as well as after the evening events. There were linens to organize, place settings to gather, groceries to purchase, candles and lights and lanterns to procure for all the guests. And someone would need to help prepare the dinners, serve the meals, wash and dry dishes regularly, find flowers for the dinner table, sweep and polish the floors and banisters, bang the carpets, wash windows, clean the commode. It was a Herculean task for anyone's skill and mind. But that was not all she had to do. There was music for church choirs, rehearsals of the oratorio society, all the while knowing full well that everyone would have a part in this major event. And what would she discuss with her guests in the groups that would gather in her home? What messages would be appropriate to convey to which guests in small conversation? And, like every woman of any age, she wondered what she would wear.

In early October, Carl took the train east to New York City to greet the guest of honor, Bishop Knut Henning Gauzelius von Schéele and Lady Anna Gustafva Maria von Schéele, whom Carl and Alma met while in Sweden in 1897. The bishop was the emissary of King Oscar II to the Swedish Lutheran churches in the United States. Carl wrote to Alma on October 6 from the New Amsterdam Hotel, 4th Avenue and 21st Street, New York:

My Dearest Alma!

The Bishop and wife, Dr. A., Rev. Ohman, Rev. Gustafson and wife of Minnesota, arrived this Sunday morning at 8:30. I got inside the lines and your greeting to Mrs. von Schéele was the first one she received in this country. She seemed a little thinner, the Bishop a little fleshier than four years ago.

I just came from the dock now, as I stand to help Dr. A with the baggage and it is now eleven o'clock. The bishop preaches at 11:30. They carry 4 trunks and 5 satchels and bags.... [Mrs. von Schéele] wears a light gray traveling dress and looked for all the world like an American lady.

I have to speak this evening, and then I take the first train home. If I don't miss connections I hope to be home Tuesday evening at Midnight, which makes it Wednesday morning at 1. Unless it rains, I will jump off at the crossing and go right to the garrette.

Lovingly, Carl[90]

Bishop and Mrs. von Schéele were honored at a dinner in the Hotel Manhattan by prominent Swedish Americans. They celebrated the bicentennial of Yale University and visited Boston, Buffalo, Lima, Ohio, and Augustana College in Rock Island. On October 23, they dined with President Theodore Roosevelt and were part of a reception attended by 500 people.[91]

With the anticipated arrival of the bishop and his wife for the November festivities, the college put the final touches on the program, and Alma worked through the most minute of details for the opening event: a dinner at the parsonage in honor of Bishop von Schéele and Mrs. von Schéele and no less than 150 guests.

With such an undertaking, Alma likely procured the assistance of people in the congregation to help with bread baking, bringing up potatoes, sweet potatoes, and vegetables from root cellars, and acquiring jellies and pickles made from the summer's bounty. Turkeys from neighboring farms were butchered and cleaned. Boullion was prepared, and lobsters were ordered specially from the East Coast for the delicacy lobster a lá Newburg (yes, they would say, one can even get lobster in Kansas). Dozens of loaves of bread were baked in the parsonage kitchen and vast trays of rolls and other delicacies added to the fragrant aroma. Water was brought to a boil in huge enamel pots on top of the kitchen stove, then coffee grounds mixed with eggs were stirred into the furiously boiling water, and the coffee was steeped to perfection. Precision, organization, skill, competency, patience, courage, and excellence were required for such an event.

The dignitaries arrived late Saturday afternoon, November 9, at the Union Pacific Depot where they were greeted by a host of horse-drawn carriages and the Bethany College Band. When the train brought the last of the visitors, the Bethany Band led the procession of carriages up town, through Main Street, to the parsonage.[92] The Bethany Band may have gathered around to serenade the guests as they stepped from their carriages, walked from Main Street and up the steps of the parsonage. And there Alma stood to warmly greet them. Her daughters and her sisters helped make the guests comfortable. The old soldier, Johan Lind, quietly stood to greet guests in another room. Mrs. Carl Anderson presided in the kitchen.

Among the guests making their way across the threshold were Bishop and Lady von Schéele; Dr. and Mrs. Abrahamson; Dr. and Mrs. M. C. Ransen of Chicago; Dr. and Mrs. Johnson of Nebraska; Col. and Mrs. C. A. Smith of Minnesota; Dr. Granville of Yale University in New Haven, Connecticut; President Andreen of the Augustana Synod, Rock Island, Illinois; State Education Superintendent, the Honorable Frank Nelson of Lindsborg; Editor Lindstrand; Mr. Norelius; Rev. and Mrs. A. M. L. Herenius; Rev. M. P. Oden; Rev. and Mrs. Olson of Paxton, Illinois. The menu provided the finest foods possible:

Bouillion   Cheesed Crackers

Lobsters a lá Newburg

French Peas   Graham Sandwiches

Roast Turkey

Browned Potatoes   Sweet Potato Croquettes

Giblet Sauce

Cranberry Jelly   Peach Pickles

Waldorf Salad

Rolls

Orange Ice   Cake

Coffee[93]

It was the most elegant meal that could possibly be served in Lindsborg, Kansas, at that time. Toasts were given to the Lutheran church, to the colleges, to Lindsborg and Kansas, to America and Sweden. Bishop von Schéele gave an address. A reporter on the scene wrote, "The evening was very delightful and Dr. and Mrs. Swensson proved themselves royal entertainers."[94]

The dinner at the parsonage was but a prelude to the twentieth anniversary celebration itself which began Sunday morning, November 10,

Guests at the Jubilee of Bethany College, November 1901. Standing: Annie Theo. Swensson, Dr. G. A. Bradelle, Dr. Abrahamson, Dr. Carl Aaron Swensson, Col. C. A. Smith, Dr. Ludwig Homes, Bertha Swensson, Jenny Lind. Seated: Dr. A. W. Dahlsten, Mrs. Brandelle, Mrs. Abrahason, Mrs. von Schéele, Dr. von Schéele, Alma Lind Swensson, Mrs. Ranseen, Mrs. C. A. Smith.

with a worship service at the college and Bishop von Schéele preaching. There is no mention of lunch, but somewhere a noon meal was served, perhaps in the college dining room.

The afternoon program began with an academic procession and addresses made in seven different languages which, the newspaper commented, was "a fine expression of the culture and knowledge of which Bethany is exponent." There was English and Swedish, of course. Professor P. H Pearson, A.M., spoke in German; Professor Birger Sandzén, A.M., French; Rev. Professor Ernst Pihlblad, A.M., Latin; Rev. Professor J. E. Eckholm, Ph.D., Greek; Rev. Professor Emil Lund, Ph.D., Hebrew. Sunday evening was graced by a double-header concert program. First, a piano recital was presented by Bethany College faculty member, Professor Sigfrid Laurin. Then, at 8:15 p.m., a concert was given by the Bethany College band, orchestra, and the *Messiah* chorus. The centerpiece of this concert was a cantata commissioned for the occasion. The music was composed by Hagbard Brasé as a setting for the words of the Rev. J. P. Sandzén, a poet, violinist, and pastor in the Church of Sweden,[95] who was the father of Professor Birger Sandzén. Soloists for the cantata were

Professors Thure Jaderborg, Sandzén, Miss Minnie Nelson, and Miss Bertha Swensson, Carl and Alma's nineteen-year-old daughter who was a gifted alto. The cornet solo "Raymond" was performed, and the evening ended with three choruses from Handel's *Messiah* performed by the Bethany Oratorio Society—"Behold the Lamb of God," "Lift Up Your Heads," and "Hallelujah." What a splendid evening it must have been as the musical gifts of the college and community were highlighted in such performances!

The program for Monday, November 11, had a student focus. Morning chapel began with a presentation by Dr. J. Tellen on higher Christian education and by State Superintendent Frank Nelson who spoke of the educational system of Kansas. Bishop von Schéele delivered a scholarly lecture on the historical development of the Christian religion. The programming for the day was adjourned early so that those who wished could watch the Bethany Terrible Fighting Swedes play the Cooper Memorial of Sterling, Kansas, at a 3:00 p.m. football game. The Swedes won under the first-year coaching of Bennie Owen, who would become the legendary coach at the University of Oklahoma. After the game, the students marched in a torchlight parade from the college, through the business district and the residences, then back to campus for a 9:00 p.m. banquet in the college dining room.

The final day of the Twentieth Anniversary Jubilee was Tuesday, November 12. The chapel service began under the leadership of the Rev. Carl Wallen, pastor of the Salemsborg congregation. At 10:30 a.m. regular Swedish anniversary exercises in the auditorium began with a congregational hymn and prayer, an anthem by the chapel choir, and the anniversary address by Bishop von Schéele on Christianity and culture. The Oratorio Society sang "Glorious Is Thy Name," and when the last notes had died away in Ling Auditorium, Bishop von Schéele unexpectedly stepped forward to make an announcement: Dr. Carl Aaron Swensson, by order of His Majesty King Oscar II, would now be knighted a member of "the Royal Order of the North Star." The entire audience rose to its feet and stood in silence while Bishop von Schéele, the king's representative, pinned the insignia on Carl's breast. Then the audience broke into resounding applause as their pastor and president thanked the bishop.[96] Perhaps he looked at Alma with thankful eyes and heart—and a good deal of pride.

But there was one more session left of the Jubilee, and that began with an address by the governor of Kansas, William Stanley, on "the Use of Modern Education," and a greeting from the Augustana Synod by Dr. Andreen, the good and dear friend of the Swenssons. In this session, Dr. Granville again brought greetings from the Yale Bethany Club and spoke of the success of the Bethany students there. Carl conferred honorary degrees on Governor Stanley; W. W. Thomas, the U.S. Minister to Sweden; George R. Peck of Chicago; J. H. Richards of Fort Scott; Charles Moreau Harger of Abilene; Major James B. Pond of New York; the Rev. C. A. Cedarstam, of Savonburg, Kansas; and Josephine Carlson Harper of Manhattan College.

Then to the amazement of all, the final benediction was given by Bishop von Schéele, not in Swedish but in English—a sign of the new future of this place.[97] Bethany had the blessing of the Swedish bishop to go forward in being an American college forged with roots and friendships in Sweden. The two greatest gifts, the old saying goes, is to give a child both roots and wings.

Their Lives to the Fullest

The final benediction had been pronounced, the dignitaries were on their way home, and the Twentieth Anniversary Jubilee continued to bring recognition to Bethany College, Bethany Church, Lindsborg, and its colossal leader, Carl Aaron Swensson.

The Messiah Festival grew to national renown. The *New York Times* reported Lindsborg "A Town *Messiah* Mad":

> A chorus of more than 500 voices and an orchestra of 60 pieces in an auditorium built especially for these annual concerts. Everyone in the little city of 2,000 inhabitants is interested in the affair. The whole ambition of the children is to become large enough to sing in *Messiah* and none are too old to take their places in the chorus, while to sing one of the leading solos is the acme of honor and fame to which there is more aspiration in Lindsborg than to become Governor of Kansas.[98]

Carl Swensson was the most recognized Swedish-American in the United States and in Sweden. His power of persuasion was immense. In 1903, for example, the Swedish government decided not to have a presence at the World's Exposition in St. Louis celebrating the centennial of the Louisiana Purchase. Carl changed their minds. He was then appointed to the building committee and may have been instrumental in suggesting that Sweden's finest architect, Ferdinand Boberg, whose buildings he and Alma saw at the Stockholm exposition in 1897, could design a pavilion suitable for St. Louis. Money had to be raised, so Carl was on the road again to Swedish-American communities in Nebraska, Iowa, Illinois, Minnesota, Wisconsin, New York, and his own Kansas. At the dedication of the building site Carl was the featured speaker on a platform filled with a host of dignitaries. Meanwhile, people in Sweden were raising money for the pavilion, too. And Boberg had a building design ready. Because this pavilion was the desire of the people and paid for with subscriptions from the people of Sweden and America, Boberg suggested a typical Swedish country manor house. It would be painted that certain Swedish yellow with white trim and a red roof. Boberg imagined that this would be where Swedish-Americans from across the country and around the world would gather to find cousins and get to know each other once again.[99]

At the same time, Bethany Lutheran Church voted to expand the sanctuary by adding two transepts, one to the east and one to the west, creating a cruciform shape. A new altar, altar railing, pulpit, lectern, baptismal font, stained glass windows, and organ would be installed. This was the opportunity to create a remarkable worship space, one unlike any other in the Augustana Synod. Perhaps Carl had memories of his father, Jonas, years ago overseeing the planning for the new church at Andover. Alma could never forget the planning of the new church at Moline while she watched the construction around her as she prepared music for worship services. Now Bethany Church, their own church, would be built on the same scale. They would ask local artists to submit bids to create a worship space with elements that would remind the congregation of Bethany, the village where Jesus gathered with his friends, and where significant events in Jesus' life occurred. The Lutheran concept of word and sacrament would be implemented with the pulpit (word) separate from the altar (sacrament).[100] It was a concept Sweden had always embraced. Carl appointed G. N. Malm, the artist, author, businessman, and designer whom he had recruited to Lindsborg from Omaha several years before, to oversee the project.

There were committee meetings to sort the details, construction workers to feed, funding to be raised throughout the parish, windows to be designed, measurements to be taken, orders to be placed, stained glass to choose. Through all of the construction, Alma conducted the choir, played for Sunday services, offered encouragement, and had a hand in deciding not only where the new organ should be placed but what it should sound like. While traveling in Omaha, Carl wrote to Alma:

> I believe your position on the place of the organ in the new church will win. It would fill too much room on the back gallery, and yet be too far away.[101]

G. N. Malm himself painted the centerpiece of the altar—Mary pouring ointment on the feet of Jesus. On either side of the altar, Birger Sandzén created larger-than-life paintings. On the pulpit side Jesus is commanding Lazarus to come out of his tomb, and on the lectern side of the altar is the ascension of Jesus.

The Palmquist brothers of Lindsborg, Alfred and August, hand-carved the altar, pulpit, baptismal font, altar railing, and lectern after Malm's design, implementing a lotus flower motif with grapes, an olive branch, the Greek signs for alpha and omega, and at the top of the altar, a simple cross. The altar, pulpit, lectern, and baptismal font were painted white and trimmed with gold leaf. The ochre sandstone, brought from the distant hills in 1874 along with dozens of loads more for the expansion, was plastered with stucco and painted white. From that time on, with the steeple soaring 125 feet in the air, Bethany church would mark the community's special place, glistening in the Kansas blue, sun-filled sky. The church would become a Lutheran cathedral and a sanctuary on the great prairie of the middle west.

At the same time, a famine gripped the northern provinces of Sweden, and, while the Lindsborg settlers were now at least a generation removed, there was concern for the people of their grandparents' homeland. The Kansas Conference raised funds for Sweden as did the entire Augustana Synod. In Lindsborg, the oratorio society gave a benefit concert. The proceeds could have gone to the church project, or to building the Swedish pavilion for the World's Fair, or to Bethany College, but it went to the starving people of northern Sweden.

And in 1903, while Carl was raising money for the Swedish pavilion, raising funding for the refurbishing of the church, bringing new faculty on board, dealing with faculty salaries and recruiting new students, and promoting the Messiah Festival, Bethany College found itself in financial difficulties. Through it all, Alma raised money for a new organ, continued as organist and choir director, welcomed guests to the parsonage, and helped reassure faculty and community and her circle of friends.

A Year of Sorrow and Singing—1904

Carl addressed a meeting of the Commercial Club once again in early January 1904, this time reporting on his successful negotiations to expand railroad service to Lindsborg. It was another one of his miracles—another community benefit that he made happen.

The great opera singer Madame Nordica gave a concert in Ling Auditorium on February 4. A massive crowd cheered the dramatic operatic star who wore a tiara and an exquisite gown. Her program included arias from *Tannhäuser* and *lieder* by Schumann, Rubinstein, Grieg, Strauss, and Gounod.[102]

And now, Carl was going to California for a speaking engagement. Dr. Abrahamson came from Chicago to join him on the trip. Abrahamson likely stayed at the parsonage, enjoying conversation at Alma and Carl's dining room table. After their guest retired for the evening and the lamp lights were turned down, Alma and Carl might have reviewed the state of affairs at Bethany College and Bethany Church before he started his extended journey: *Messiah* rehearsals were already underway. The first performance would be Palm Sunday, March 27. Easter Sunday would be April 3. The art department had their plans in place for the annual exhibition of work by students and faculty—another dimension added to Messiah Festival week in 1899 by Sandzén, Lotave, and Malm. At Bethany Church Alma was preparing the choir for the anthems to be sung at services during Lent and Holy Week. Carl would work on his sermons during the long train trip. The building project at the church was coming along nicely and looked to be completed in time for the June meeting of the Augustana Synod. And of course the Augustana Women's Missionary Society met at the same time when Alma would help preside at their meeting as recording secretary. She had already begun work on hospitality for the hundreds of people expected at the annual gathering. At the college, the financial situation had evened out a bit, and Carl hoped to raise additional money on this trip west. Classes were at the mid-point in the academic year. The music department was preparing for spring recitals to be given by students after Easter. And their daughters, Bertha, now twenty-two, and Annie, twenty, were doing well themselves. Carl and Alma were proud of their daughters who were talented, graceful, and still filled with the enthusiasm of youth.

In the morning after breakfast, Alma said her good bye to Carl, then he and Dr. Abrahamson made their way to the train depot.

Alma turned to her duties as organist and choir director, making sure that all was in order for the coming Sunday services. She corresponded with Emmy Evald and all the others through her responsibilities she carried with the Women's Missionary Society both on a local and synodical level. Jenny Lind, Alma's sister and Carl's secretary, kept her duties as assigned, and all waited to hear from Carl and the fruits of his speeches.

Alma received a letter dated February 12, 1904, and postmarked San Francisco. Lottie Swenson, one of her Women's Missionary Society friends wrote:

> I wanted to tell you what good luck I had: I heard Dr. Swensson preach three times last Sunday. Now I suppose that you seldom hear him that many times in one day. I did enjoy the day so much. Dr. Swensson told me you were adding to the church building in Lindsborg to be ready for the Synod meeting. My, what a busy time you will have again and just at that time when you all have more than enough to do without any extra.[103]

On Monday, February 15, Alma received a telegram informing her to come at once to Los Angeles. Carl was in Angel's Hospital, suffering from pneumonia. She quickly got things in order, packed a small bag, and boarded the train. When the train reached Newton, just a few miles down the track, she received shocking news. Carl had died. This great, robust, larger-than-life man, her husband, her partner, was dead. He was forty-six years old.

Alma returned to Lindsborg. A funeral had to be planned.

In the meantime, newspapers in Los Angeles, Denver, Chicago, Kansas City, St. Louis, San Francisco, and Topeka caught the wire services: "1:30 a.m., February 16, 1904. Dr. Carl Aaron Swensson is dead. The great Colossus of the Plains is dead." The Swedish-American newspapers *Svenska Tribunen, Hemlandet,* and *Nordstjeranan* carried the headline: *"Dr. Swensson är Död."*

The word went out to churches throughout the country, to church leaders Norelius and Andreen, to Brandelle and Wahlstrom, to Carl's brother John in New York, to their great friend Colonel Smith in Minneapolis, to the World's Fair Committee in St. Louis, to Ambassador Thomas in Stockholm, to Bishop von Schéele in Visby.

And all through the town and all through the college campus, there was stunned silence.

On Friday afternoon, February 19, faculty and students assembled on Bethany's campus and marched en masse to the depot to wait for the Union Pacific bearing the body of their founder and president. The train slowly pulled in and came to a stop. The casket was carefully lifted from its resting place and brought out from the train into the mid-afternoon sunlight. The pallbearers carried the casket between two columns formed by members of the Commercial Club.

People stood in hushed silence along the route. They heard the sound of horses' hooves against the packed earth of Main Street. The stores and businesses, draped in black, were closed. The Bethany Band played a funeral dirge, leading the procession on the same route where, just three years before, a parade of carriages brought a host of dignitaries to celebrate the Bethany College Jubilee. The procession passed by Bethany Church, the great cathedral church, and stopped at the parsonage. The music continued while the casket was removed, and Carl's body was lovingly received by those who had waited—Alma, Bertha, Annie, Jenny, Nora, Herman, Carl's brothers John and Luther, his sister Anna Maria. The old soldier, Johan, almost eighty-nine, likely wore his medal from the king to honor his son-in-law. As was the custom of the time, the body was kept in the parsonage for vigil and prayers. Friends, colleagues, and parishioners came to call at the parsonage over the weekend and through Monday to express their sympathy and disbelief. No doubt someone in the kitchen made coffee and prepared food for those who called. Perhaps Alma was expected to host overnight guests arriving from Illinois, New York, Minnesota, Colorado, and Nebraska.

The morning of the funeral, Tuesday, February 23, dawned bright, brisk, and invigorating. "It is a Carl Aaron Swensson sort of day," someone was heard to remark. Pallbearers brought the body to Ling Auditorium where it lay in state from 9:00 a.m. to 1:00 p.m. upon a draped catafalque set among hundreds of floral displays. A sun sculpture was placed at the casket's head; garlands of leaves entwined the auditorium's pillars. The newspaper reported that "thousands of people thronged the auditorium to cast a last look upon Dr. Swensson's face. It was a wonderful outpouring of the people's sympathy. Nothing like it has ever been seen in Kansas."[104]

At 1:00 p.m., the body was brought again to the home for a private family service led by Dr. W. Dahlsten and Rev. Dr. P. P. Lindal. The church choir, Alma's choir, sang an anthem, as did the male chorus. The pallbearers returned to bring the casket to Ling Auditorium for the final service. The casket was carried in to a funeral march played on the organ by Professor Hagbard Brasé. The audience numbered 2,500 along with the 600-member choir and forty-five-piece orchestra. Sermons were given, memorials read, anthems were sung, a telegraph was read from President Teddy Roosevelt. Dr. Weidner, in his address, stated that the American flag at the Swedish Legation at Stockholm was flying at half-mast.[105]

At the end of the service, the Bethany Oratorio Society sang "Worthy Is the Lamb" and the "Amen" from *Messiah*. Next the Bethany orchestra played a funeral dirge as the casket was carried out of the auditorium to the hearse where two black horses stood ready to lead a mile-long procession to Elmwood Cemetery. There the final rites were spoken. The benediction was said, and the casket was lowered into the Kansas earth. All of those assembled joined in singing Carl's favorite hymn, "Nearer, My God, to Thee." Night fell upon Lindsborg; but the faith of a Christian people rested them in the hopes of the morning.[106]

The Messiah Festival of 1904 went on as scheduled. Carl would have wanted it, Alma was sure of that. Did she sing with the Oratorio Society that year? The opportunity to sing the music that was such a part of her life may have been the outlet she needed to express the inexpressible emotions of her grief. Since her marriage to Carl, her life had been lived in a veritable fish bowl. Her every move watched carefully since the moment she stepped from the train on that September day in 1880, the young pastor's bride. Now, in this very public performance, she could blend in with others, and she could find a way to express her deepest emotions through the music. Quietly, perhaps, and without fanfare, she took her place in the soprano section among the people with whom she had been singing for twenty-two years.

As scheduled, the Augustana Synod held its forty-fifth annual convention at Bethany Church June 2 to 7. With 300 delegates and more than 200 visitors, it was one of the most well-attended in the synod's history. The newly expanded Bethany Church sanctuary was finished and enhanced with work by Lindsborg's own artists. A new pipe organ supported the hymn singing, and there was nothing quite like a gathering of Lutherans for singing. Alma and Carl had envisioned this.

The synod opened on Thursday evening. The great church leader, Dr. Eric Norelius, one of the founders of the Augustana Synod and now serving his second term as president, was in the pulpit and would preside over the entire series of meetings. Rev. Ernst Pihlblad extended the delegates and guests welcome to Bethany Church and to the Lindsborg community. Dr. J. V. Kildahl, a delegate from the United Norwegian Lutheran Church, urged a closer union of Lutheran church forces.

Friday morning, the business sessions of the synod opened at Bethany Chapel with full attendance and hosts of visitors, members of the theological seminary at Rock Island, Bethany College faculty, visiting clergy, and the mayor of Lindsborg.

Saturday, there was the round of synod reports. In the evening, the Lindsborg Commercial Club gave a banquet and reception at the college dining hall with toasts all around. Sunday, fully 2,000 people attended morning and afternoon services where twenty-nine young men were ordained for the ministry. That evening, reports were received regarding the synod's work with youth. A concert was presented by the choir and by Bertha Swensson.

On Monday afternoon, at 4:30 p.m., the entire Synod—some 500 people—marched the mile-long road west to Elmwood Cemetery to pay tribute at Carl's grave. Dr. Norelius spoke. Poems were read by Dr. Stolpe and Dr. Hemborg. At the end of the program, all 500 voices joined in singing "Nearer, My God, to Thee." The delegates and visitors made their way back to campus where they ate dinner in the dining room.

Monday evening, the Augustana Women's Missionary Society, which met concurrently with the synod, held its own tribute to Carl. A correspondent for the Lindsborg *News* describes the program:

> Mrs. Emmy Evald made an interesting address. On the platform opposite the pulpit was a bust of the late Dr. Swensson, the friend of the Missionary Society. At the close of Mrs. Evald's address, representative ladies from each conference in the Synod stepped forward and placed a wreath of flowers upon the Dr. Swensson bust. It was a tender, touching, gracious, and beautiful testimony of the love and esteem in which the Society holds the service and memory of Dr. Swensson.[107]

Bertha Swensson, Vendla Wetterstrom, and Mellicent Thorstenberg furnished beautiful music. Alma was re-elected recording secretary.

PHOTO BY B. G. GRÖNDAL

Johan Lind, father of Alma Lind Swensson.

The synod meeting was over. Alma had endured this second enormously public event without Carl. Then two weeks later, Alma bore another loss in her life. Her father, Johan Lind, the old soldier, died at Alma's home on June 23. "Mr. Lind served with honor and distinction in the Swedish army, having enlisted in 1842," the Lindsborg *News* reported. Funeral services were held Monday afternoon, June 27, from Bethany Church. His children—Herman, Alma, Nora, and Jenny, and three grandchildren—Bertha, Annie, and Esther survive. "At Rest" read the headline in the newspaper on July 1, 1904. He was buried beside his wife, not far from Carl's grave, in Elmwood Cemetery.

On Her Own

The partnership ended with Carl's death. Alma may have asked herself, "Now what?" She had been a confidante to her husband who was pastor of the large congregation, president of the growing college, and a national leader in education, church, and Swedish-American culture. What was her position in this place on the Kansas prairie? What was in store for her, for Bethany Church and Bethany College?

From a twenty-first-century perspective, one believes that Alma could have administered the college, could have run the press, and kept the correspondence with Swedish bishops and archbishops. She could have made sure the pavilion at the St. Louis World's Fair would run smoothly and would have gladly stood at the door welcoming those long-lost cousins trying to find each other. But in the early twentieth century there were still conventions women had to acknowledge.

Two men were selected to succeed Carl in the work he had begun. Dr. Ernst Pihlblad, vice president of Bethany College and assistant pastor of Bethany Church, was soon elected by the synod as the new president of the college. Dr. Alfred Bergin of Cambridge, Minnesota, was called by the congregation of Bethany Church to be the new pastor. He would move into the parsonage in November with his wife, Anna, and young daughters, Adele, Ruth, and Esther.

And so Alma spent the golden autumn months packing away the books, music, dishes, candelabra—all that she had used to entertain heads of state, senators, bishops, archbishops, singers, alumni, the Women's Missionary Society—every remembrance of her life with Carl. According to protocol, she sent back to Sweden the Royal Order of the North Star—back to the king, whose emissary had knighted her husband that day in 1901 as 2,000 people in Ling Auditorium stood in respectful silence when the Bishop of Visby pinned the order on Carl's academic gown.

Now Alma closed the door to the large, beautiful parsonage that had been their home. All but her basic necessities were in storage. She walked across the street to the women's college dormitory and took up residence in two rooms. Alma Christina Lind Swensson, in the space of eight months, lost her husband, her father, her home, and her position in the community. But life for Alma would go on. She was still the organist of Bethany Church and the choir director. It was time to get the choir ready for Advent and Christmas.

During the early, darkest hours before dawn on Christmas morning, 1904, Alma made her way from the empty women's dormitory to the church, music in her satchel, ready for *Julotta*. Frost swayed on the branches and caught the rays from candle lamps placed in the windows along the way, glowing softly to ward off the darkness and the chill. *Julotta* began at 5:00 a.m. with her organ solo. Then she directed the church choir in an anthem for the dawning of Christmas Day. The new pastor, Dr. Bergin, conducted the service before a full capacity congregation. "*Helig, helig, helig är Herren Sebaot. Hela jorden är full av hans härlighet,*" Dr. Bergin intoned. The Lindsborg *Record* reported: "The powerful sermon, the mighty chorales, the hundreds of candles, the beautiful choir, the vast audience, all helped to make the service one long to be remembered."[108]

The year 1905 must have been very difficult for Alma who had to come to terms with the struggle and loss of her husband and father and home. The oratorio society may have sustained her. People had not lost their enthusiasm for the twice-weekly rehearsals, and the Oratorio Society had grown to more than 500 members. This would be an enduring

Bethany Lutheran Church.

legacy to both Alma and Carl. Another legacy was announced in March when word was received that Boberg's Swedish Pavilion at the St. Louis World's Fair had been purchased by W. W. Thomas, the American minister to Sweden, and given to Bethany College in honor and memory of his friend, Carl Aaron Swensson. The pavilion would house a museum and the art department.[109]

Alma's work as recording secretary of the Women's Missionary Society brought her in communication with women of similar interests and purposes across the country—including her dear friend Emmy Evald. She travelled to the Women's Missionary Society's meetings, which were held in conjunction with the synod, and so there was opportunity for her to visit with Carl's friends and colleagues while focusing her own energy to the interest of the organization for which she was so instrumental from the beginning.

On July 7, 1905, Bethany Church notes in the Lindsborg *News* that "Mrs. Swensson left last Monday for a couple of months rest and sojourn in the East." She decided to take a break. And as she east traveled by train, she could well have recalled the last eighteen months. She herself had carried on as well as possible. The new pastor of Bethany Church, Dr. Alfred Bergin, was comfortably in place. The new college president, Dr. Ernst Pihlblad, a protegé of Carl's, had taken that yoke of responsibility. The church refurbishment—the hand-carved pulpit, altar, baptismal font, lectern, and the windows and paintings—was completed and as beautiful as she and Carl could ever have imagined. The synod had been warmly welcomed to its meeting in 1904 by the people of Bethany Church as had the Women's Missionary Society. Both bodies had paid moving tribute to Carl.

And now, she felt she could take a break.

A sojourn east. Did this mean a trip to Jamestown, New York, to visit her brother-in-law, John? Perhaps she stopped in Andover, the place of her first American home. Perhaps she stopped at Moline, the old home where she and her siblings played together as children and grew up together in the old neighborhood. Perhaps she sat in the pew of the Swedish Lutheran Church and remembered that it was here that she was named organist at the tender age of twelve. These places and memories would have touched her heart—points along the journey before her life with Carl.

Perhaps Alma spent time in Chicago with Emmy Evald, the president of the Augustana Women's Missionary Society. Emmy may have shared an idea that she had been mulling over for some time. The Women's Missionary Society had just finished its thirteenth annual meeting. Members were now spread across the country, and they needed a system to keep them connected—a formal newsletter that would remind them, encourage them, and report on the work that was happening all over the world. Emmy, conscious of the possibilities of women working together, may have thought that there could be no one better to edit this newsletter than the thoughtful, articulate, extremely capable, eminently qualified, and highly respected Alma Swensson. Perhaps Alma spent time with Emmy during the sojourn, and Emmy presented her with this offer. "Alma," she might have said, "You can help bring us together. You can connect us each month by reporting on the work, encouraging and updating all the chapters. This would be a great service to the church and to women everywhere. You, Alma, are perfect."

Alma considered it and then agreed to Emmy's encouragement and invitation. The first issue appeared in 1906 at the Women's Missionary Society/synod meeting in Denver with Alma's name as editor-in-chief. The title of the paper was *Missions-Tidning*, and both she and the paper received a very warm reception at its presentation.

A Home of Her Own

In May 1907, the Lindsborg *Record* notes that "Mrs. Dr. Swensson is having the goods moved from the storeroom at Bethany Flats into her new home recently purchased on College Street."[110] Three years after she left the parsonage, she was moving into a home of her own. The house had been owned by a friend of Carl's—Charles Lander, a farmer, stockman, president of the commercial club, and mayor of Lindsborg from 1893 to 1898. Mr. Lander was elected to the Kansas State House in 1905 and again in 1907. Her new home was a three-story Queen Anne with wrap-around porches and a pediment above the front door. Built in 1877 and directly across the street from the Bethany campus, it was just a block from Bethany Church. The setting for Alma was perfect.

PHOTO BY KAREN A. HUMPHREY.

Alma Swensson's House. Alma lived here from 1907 to 1939.

The home's front door, with a leaded glass window, opened to a small front hall and a curving staircase to the top floors where four bedrooms would provide room for herself and her guests. From her own bedroom, if she looked in just the right direction, she would see the heroic white marble statue of Carl in front of the Main Building, created in Italy and dedicated at Bethany College in April 1907. The third floor had additional bedrooms. A back stairway went to the large kitchen where there was a coal stove, an icebox, large table, pantry, and a door to a porch facing north. The dining room had a matching buffet and china cupboard built in the wall with a serving space below the cabinet and glass doors that opened into the kitchen. The library had floor to ceiling bookshelves, a black leather sofa, rocking chairs, a piano, and a library table in the center of the room with a large Boston fern on a pedestal. The living room was called "the front room" with a love seat, a wooden rocker, and chairs upholstered in green. Between the rooms, the doorways were hung with heavy green portieres.[111] Here she would be at home for the rest of her life, and the house would be forever known in Lindsborg as Alma Swensson's house.

The move to her new home coincided with the marriage of her oldest daughter, Bertha, to Axel Vestling in late June 1907. The wedding was an occasion filled with flowers, music, friends, and memories—likely the happiest event of the new century. Bertha and Axel, whose late father was also a pastor, graduated in the same class at Bethany College in 1904. Axel was one of those Bethany alums who went to Yale, earning his Ph.D. in German the spring of 1907. Bertha pursued voice studies in Chicago.

The wedding was held at 8:00 p.m. at Bethany Church, which was "tastefully and prettily decorated for the occasion in green and white." Dr. Hagbard Brasé played an organ recital while more than 400 guests were seated by six ushers, including Bertha's uncles Herman Lind, George Eberhardt, and Eben Carlsson. The flower girl, Miriam Hult of Chicago, wore a white net over pink silk, and carried a basketful of pink roses. Annie was her sister's bridesmaid and was dressed in white net over white taffeta. She held a bouquet of pink roses. Then the bride, Bertha Maria Fredrika, carrying a bouquet of lilies of the valley, came in on the arm of her mother. The wedding gown was white mousseline de sole over white chiffon taffeta, and the bride wore a diamond brooch—a gift of the groom. Alma was dressed in white crepe de Chine over white silk. Alma walked Bertha down the aisle of Bethany Church, lined with white columns entwined with smilax and joined with white festoons. Bethany College President Dr. Ernst Pihlblad and the pastor of Bethany Church, Dr. Alfred Bergin, waited at the altar where the bride and groom met under an arch, prepared especially for the occasion and anchored with palm branches and ferns. Here Alma gave her daughter's hand to Dr. Vestling and, in doing so, received a thoughtful, intellectual son-in-law.

Following the ceremony, the guests made their way to Ling Auditorium where a three-course dinner was served. They were entertained by the male chorus, the orchestra, and soprano solos sung by Myrtle Sundstrom. After the toasts were made, poems read, and telegrams and greetings shared, the bride and groom, their family and closest friends were invited to Alma's new home for further refreshments. At 2:30 a.m., a procession of carriages made their way to the depot where a large crowd wished the newlyweds Godspeed, and the male chorus serenaded the Vestlings as they boarded the train for Axel's hometown, Luddington, Michigan. From there they would go to Buffalo and Jamestown, New York, to visit Bertha's uncle and aunt, and finally to New Haven, Connecticut, where Axel would begin his position at Yale as an instructor in German.[112]

Alma's new home was the scene of another gathering of friends and family on the warm Kansas summer evening of July 2. The Lindsborg *Record* published the story on its front page:

> On last Tuesday evening, the pleasant home of Mrs. Carl Swensson was the scene of a happy event in the nature of an informal reception given by Mrs. Swensson in honor of her visiting guests, Mr. and Mrs. Oscar Blomgren, of Cambridge, Illinois; Miss Cederstam, of Olsburg, Kansas; and Mr. Emil Verner of Minneapolis, Minnesota. There were present about seventy-five guests, who upon their arrival at the home were pleasantly introduced by the hostess to her guests of honor. The exchange of greetings being over, light refreshments were served in the open—on the porches and on the lawn, the guests being seated at tables. Mrs. Swensson in a few well-chosen words, making kindly mention of her guests of honor, and expressing her gratitude for once more having been placed in a position

to entertain in a home of her own, introduced the toastmaster of the evening—president Ernst F. Pihlblad, who in his usual happy way introduced the various speakers. Professors Birger Sandzén, P. H. Pearson, Emil Verner, Frank Nelson, Dr. Alf. Bergin, and Rev. Malm spoke in the order mentioned. Prof. Pihlblad closed with prayer, invoking God's blessing upon the hostess, on the evening and on her newly established home. The Male Chorus and Prof. Lofgren gave beautiful renditions of song and music. Truly, as one of the speakers happily remarked, some of our dearest Lindsborg memories are linked, in one way or another, with the Swensson home, and the event of last Tuesday evening will long be dearly cherished by those who were present.[113]

Alma had established herself and was making her way. She discovered she was independent, now, of the role of "pastor's wife" or "wife of 'our' college president," though she would most often be referred to as Mrs. Dr. Swensson. But she had titles and responsibilities of her own: church organist, editor-in-chief, choral conductor, founder of the Bethany Oratorio Society, recording secretary and co-founder of the Augustana Women's Missionary Society, vice-president of the Oratorio Society. She brought people together to do things they could not imagine doing, and she helped lift their vision of accomplishment. A new chapter in her life journey had begun.

In 1907, Annie made Lindsborg her permanent home. A graduate of Bethany College and of graduate studies at Columbia School of Expression in Chicago, she had been hired by Bethany College to teach elocution, drama, and to coach plays for the college. She lived with her mother, and the two of them would be companions for the next thirty-two years. On June 6, 1913, Alma received a new title, that of grandmother. Twins, a boy and a girl, were born to Bertha and Axel in Northfield, Minnesota, where Axel was now dean at Carleton College. The twins were named Bertha Louise and Carl Swensson Vestling.

Alma had many things to do. On March 16, 1912, Alma represented the Womans Society of Cemetery Improvements at a meeting of the Lindsborg Cemetery Company. She gave a short talk comparing the growth of the city at that time and thirty years earlier, when she and Carl first arrived in Lindsborg. She spoke of the modern and up-to-date houses, the large businesses and well-kept streets, and the beautiful and large trees where there had been none before. But the cemetery, Alma declared in her speech, had not been improved and made more beautiful in the same proportion with the growth of the city. Her suggestion, on behalf of the Womans Society, was to combine efforts. She recommended that each lot owner be solicited for $1.00 each year for fixing up the cemetery grounds. The Womans Society had already begun the work and was planning a dinner to be served on Memorial Day, with all the proceeds going toward beautifying the cemetery. In addition, on behalf of the Womans Society, she suggested that a competent man be hired for five to six months to care for the cemetery grounds.

One cannot help but think the Lindsborg Cemetery Company was impressed, for a week later Alma was elected to the cemetery board. Two weeks later, she was elected vice president. And in 1919, Alma was elected president—a post she held for eleven years. During her board tenure, the association erected an entrance gate, five settees were placed in the cemetery, and flowers, shrubs, and trees were planted. A shelter house also was built.[114]

During Holy Week, 1912, the Bethany Oratorio Society honored Alma with a special gold medal. G. N. Malm designed the medal commemorating the thirtieth anniversary of the first performance of *Messiah*. On one side the medal showed a woman sowing grain and a man harvesting a crop surrounded by the saying, in Greek, "One Sows Another Reaps." The opposite side carried the simple heartfelt inscription: "To Its First Leader, Mrs. Carl Swensson, From the Bethany Oratorio Society." The medal hung on a silk ribbon of Bethany blue and gold.

Alma's home became the center of family celebrations. Her niece, Elinor Lind Gahnstrom, born in 1907, recalled Christmas Eve at Aunt Alma's:

> Mama, Papa [Herman Lind—Alma's brother] and I would walk to her house through the crunching snow under the moonlight carrying a big laundry basket full of gifts. When we entered their door, we were ushered into the library where the green portieres to the living room would be tightly closed, and none of the children would dare to peek between them.

Aunt Nora and Uncle George would be there with my cousins Leroy, Carl and Johnny, and sometimes Aunt Jenny. We would all go first to the dining room where there would be a beautifully set table full of wonderful food. I remember one time there was a very beautiful pink dish that Aunt Nora made. I couldn't wait to try it but when I tasted it, it was made of beets and whipped cream and it was terrible! After we had eaten, we would all go into the library, where we would visit until the dishes were done.

Then Aunt Alma would announce that we could go to the living room where there was a beautiful Christmas tree. In the first years, it was lit with candles and then later with electric lights. Someone would be assigned to be Santa Claus. Most often it was one of the boys but sometimes Papa would be Santa and I would help him. The one Christmas we had with my little brother Howard, who was one month old, we both got beautiful baby dolls just alike with complete outfits that Aunt Nora had ordered from a dressmaker.

On Christmas day morning, *Julotta*, it was a must that we would arise at 4 a.m. upon hearing the band playing in the steeple of Bethany Church. It was cold, so their instruments were out of tune, but we tho't the music beautiful. As we walked towards church through the snow, every house had a big, lit candle glowing in a window.[115]

Elinor recalled that she would often accompany her father to visit Alma, and they would discuss, sometimes quite vehemently, affairs of world interest. Elinor remembered that her Aunt Alma took principled stands for women's suffrage as well as human rights. When asked to host Kansas Governor Henry Allen overnight, Alma was incensed that his chauffeur, who was black, was not allowed to stay in Lindsborg because of the color of his skin, and she offered him a room at her house.[116] "She became very disillusioned when the powers that be told her he couldn't stay there but would have to go to Salina for the night," Elinor wrote. "This is just one instance in which she voiced her very strong opinion of injustice."

Often the discussions between Alma and her brother, Herman, centered on what was happening at the college, economic problems of the country, concerns of family members. "Sometimes they would just have an evening of recalling their childhood, old friends, and relatives," Elinor remembered. Then the brother and sister would change from English to Swedish, "not because they didn't want me to understand but simply it seemed to me it was more appropriate to use their old language when reviewing the old times."[117]

Many times, when she would drop in to visit her Aunt Alma, Elinor would find the large dining room table covered with books, notes, and articles she was writing for *Missions-Tidning*. "She had a deadline to meet," Elinor recalled, "and would often scurry out the door well after midnight to rush down to the railway station with her material which must go on the Flyer so it would reach Rock Island in time."

Alma's World View

Her work as editor-in-chief of *Missions-Tidning* meant ever more to Alma and brought a broad, international perspective to her home at 343 First Street in Lindsborg. Through the magazine she connected Augustana missionaries serving around the world to Augustana Lutheran women across the country, all the while fulfilling the paper's emphasis on educating people about the work of church missions. Her communication with missionaries gave her an outlook and viewpoint that few others could have. The magazine she edited would be her voice in telling of the work of the church, and *Missions-Tidning* would be of central importance to the Augustana Women's Missionary Society.[118]

That first issue of *Missions-Tidning*, presented in 1906 at the convention in Denver, told the story of accomplishments during the fourteen years since the Augustana Women's Missionary Society was organized at her parsonage home. The first issue announced that more than $25,000 had been raised for such mission projects as famine relief in India, the acquisition of a hospital site in India, missions in Puerto Rico, in China, and tuition for Betty Nilsson who was studying to be a medical doctor. At first the magazine was published quarterly. Two years later, when *Missions-Tidning* became a monthly publication, Alma's work became almost full-time.[119]

In her mail each week Alma opened dispatches from missionaries serving across oceans, seas, and continents detailing their work—of building a school for girls in the Hunan Province of China; a home for widows and a hospital for women and children in Rajahmundry, India; missions for new immigrants on Ellis Island; missions in Jerusalem; reports from Palestine; updates on missions among the Jews of Philadelphia; progress on fundraising for French war orphans.

As editor of *Missions-Tidning*, she reached a monthly audience of up to 25,000 people in all parts of the United States.[120] Wherever Augustana

Lutheran women lived—in farm homes on the sprawling prairies; in brownstones and apartments in large cities; in rural parsonages, village homes, and college communities of all sizes—Alma's newsletters were in their hands, and they read of missionaries' work around the globe. Alma told how they became involved in each other's lives through prayer, intercession, story telling, fundraising, and practical work on the mission field. Readers followed the efforts of missionary teacher May Mellander in Puerto Rico; Sister Ingeborg Nystul, a medical and evangelistic worker in China; Dr. Lydia Woerner in India; Dr. Betty Nilsson, Dr. Woerner's successor in Rajahmundry; Signe Ekblad in Jerusalem; Mrs. Hobart Johnson in Africa; Hilda Andersson in Palestine. Alma included in the magazine mission studies to be used in local group meetings, short dramas that could be acted by young people, poetry, commentary by the Women's Missionary Society President Emmy Evald, and fundraising appeals on behalf of mission work.

And from the Augustana conferences throughout the United States—from the Red River Valley of North and South Dakota, from Iowa, Minnesota, Illinois, New York, New England, California, the Pacific Northwest, the Rocky Mountains, Texas, Michigan, Nebraska, and Kansas—came reports of individual congregational activities.

In 1909 Alma connected women beyond the missionary fields of Africa, China, and India when Lutheran women of Sweden, Denmark, Norway, Finland, and Germany joined the Women's Missionary Society in establishing the First Sunday in Advent as a Day of Prayer for Missions. Indeed, the work of the Women's Missionary Society had a global impact, and Alma was the one who told the story. She began a special page for children in 1909 to share stories of young people who were served by Augustana missionaries. In 1912 an English section was added.[121] Alma continued to edit the Swedish section for another twenty-seven years.[122]

As editor-in-chief Alma traveled from Lindsborg to the synodical conventions each year, in such places as Chicago, Illinois; Jamestown, New York; New Britain, Connecticut; Minneapolis, St. Paul, Duluth, and Red Wing, Minnesota. At the synodical gatherings she joined hundreds of women committed to the work of church mission.

The Women's Missionary Society gathered in Rock Island to celebrate their silver jubilee in 1917. After Emmy Evald recalled the beginnings of their organization at the parsonage in Lindsborg, she was presented with "a bouquet of words." In essence these were Alma's words that described the work of women who shared the passion for the command to "Go, Tell." The Women's Missionary Society also honored Alma with a tribute for her twenty-five years of "faithful and fruitful service in the Society since its organization." She did not seek re-election to the post of recording secretary, but continued as editor-in-chief of the magazine.[123]

The Augustana Synod met again in Lindsborg, July 12 to 17, 1919, fifteen years after that momentous year, 1904. The tenth anniversary of *Missions-Tidning* was celebrated with a "birthday surprise party." At the end of the Women's Missionary Society meeting, Alma surprised her friends by hosting a reception at her home in honor of the charter members and their daughters also attending the convention. A photo taken of the group shows nine of the founding members, including Alma's sisters Jenny Lind and Nora Lind Eberhardt, her friends Ellen Wikstrand, Hilma Weline, Anna Dahlsten, Uma Bersell, and the central figure of the society, Emmy Evald. In the photo Alma is sixty years old. Still erect, tall, slender, with silver hair, she is wearing a white summer dress and appears to have her arm around Emmy, her friend, confidante, and colleague.[124] Hospitality was still golden at Alma's house.

Alma wanted her readers to remember their own mothers and sisters, who like many mothers in Africa, China, and India lived lives of sacrifice,

The Women's Missionary Society, 1919. Alma is seated fourth from the left, in a white dress, with her arm around Emmy Evald, the dynamic president of the society.

devotion, and courage. "Oh, if we had a history of this noble band of women. We children have neglected to gather facts and experiences. Let us, though it is late, gather in writing and print what we remember of them." The May 1924 issue of *Missions-Tidning* carried the stories of fifteen pioneer mothers and, perhaps for the first time in printed material, the full names of the women are given and there is a sense of their own identity: Amalia Marie Louisa Planting, Gyllenbåga Esbjorn, Johanna Laurentia LeVeau Cederstam, Hilda Esping Andreen, Charlotta Ornstedt-Sjöblom, Eva Helena Cervin Hasselquist, Eva Charlotta Anderson Carlsson.[125]

All throughout her thirty-one year career as editor-in-chief, Alma promoted the women's work on the mission field, women supporting women on the mission field, and women working together in country-crossroad congregations as well as in metropolitan areas such as Brooklyn, Philadelphia, Chicago, and Tacoma. Alma's own mission through *Missions-Tidning*, from Matthew 28:10, as the risen Christ commanded Mary and Mary Magdalene: "Go and tell."

Ever Greater: "Her" Festival

The Bethany Oratorio Society gained ever greater renown. Internationally acclaimed musicians and operatic singers came to Lindsborg to perform during the Messiah Festival. Madame Ernestine Schumann-Heink, Madame Lillian Nordica, Galli-Curci, Gadski, Marian Talley, Jennie Tourel, Efrem Zimbalist, Eugène Ysaÿe, Gregor Piatigorsky, and Isaac Stern all graced the Ling Auditorium stage at Bethany College and filled the auditorium with people hungry for gorgeous music. But in the spring of 1918, the Oratorio Society took its own gorgeous music east to Camp Funston, Kansas, for two special performances.[126]

On May 13, 1918, the Oratorio Society and orchestra boarded a special train with eleven coaches to Camp Funston where the 89th Division was preparing to go to the World War I battlefields of Europe. Most of the soldiers in training were from farms, country crossroads, and villages in Colorado, Missouri, Nebraska, South Dakota, New Mexico, and Kansas. The Oratorio Society sang *Messiah* twice that day for 8,000 soldiers who were dressed in their khaki uniforms. Just weeks later, the 89th Division headed to Esseg, Beney, Croatia, Boullionville, Pannes, and Xanvers in France, and then to Bitburg, Trier, and Saarburg in Germany where they encountered the horrors and heroism of war.

During commencement ceremonies in 1922, Bethany College awarded Alma an Honorary Doctor of Humane Letters in recognition of her accomplishments and her service to the church and the college. Also receiving honorary doctorate honors that day were Dr. C. A. John, head of research at Standard Oil Company, and Alma's old friend and the college's first professor, Dr. Johan August Udden, now of Austin, Texas, and an internationally respected geologist.

A reporter for the *New York Times* wrote on November 12, 1922:

Seeing the "Messiah" chorus grow from a little country church choir to the nationally known chorus of 1922, says the *Kansas City Star*, which brings thousands of people from out of the State into the Lindsborg landscape annually that they may hear it—that is the experience of Mrs. Alma Swensson, first director of the organization. Mrs. Swensson, wife of Dr. Carl Swensson, founder of Bethany College, is the Vice President of the Oratorio Society. She holds the unusual distinction of having sung in each of the 119 renditions of Handel's masterpiece by the Lindsborg choir.[127]

PHOTO BY B. G. GRÖNDAL

The most familiar portrait of Alma Lind Swensson.

While Alma had never directed the choir in performance, she was, indeed the first director.[128] News reporters from around the country, when writing about the Oratorio Society and the Messiah Festival, now called it "her festival"—meaning Alma's. Another *Times* reporter wrote that the 500 singers presented a typical cross-section of the Swedish-American farming community: "Frequently three generations of a family are represented. In the soprano section is Mrs. Alma Swensson, widow of the preacher who founded the organization fifty-four years ago. She will sing again this year as she has ever since the little community started building its great musical organization."[129]

Another reporter contacted Dr. Udden, and asked how an organization could find success in such a small town. Udden replied, "It was this little woman's [sic] talent and tenacious energy plus Dr. Swensson's charming personality that made the Messiah Chorus a possibility in Lindsborg."

Alma had a chance to tell the story of the Messiah Festival to a reporter from *The New York Times* in 1923.

When we came to these unbroken prairies forty years ago, there were, counting most of the families within driving distance, not more than two hundred persons. There was not much musical ability; nor was there any outstanding religious feeling out of which the singing of a great religious oratorio might grow. On the contrary, we found only a few country boys and girls, much more used to their heavy farm tasks than to the delicacy of tone discrimination.

The reason for the annual Messiah Festival is just this, Dr. Swensson wanted it. He was a man of ideals and vision. Once, in Moline, Illinois, he had heard parts of the oratorio, and in his youthful enthusiasm for Kansas he wanted the beauty and spiritual power of that music built into this community. I knew a little about music, and I wanted more than anything else for him to have what he wanted.[130]

The headline declared: "Lindsborg: The American Oberammergau on the Plains of Kansas."

During the fifty-eighth year of its presentation of *Messiah* in 1930, the National Broadcasting Company carried selected choruses from *Messiah* to millions of listeners throughout the country across the blue network. The occasion noted was the celebration of a quarter century "of noble and inspiring service to the cause of music in the community by Dr. Hagbard Brasé."[131] No one needed to remind any of the musicians or most of the community that it was Alma who prepared the choir in the first place.

In April 1939, *Time* magazine's music section began a story called "The Wheat Belt Messiah" with Alma's name in the lead:

Alma Swensson was the prim, capable wife of a Lutheran schoolman in the little Swedish-American town of Lindsborg, Kansas (pop. 2,004). Alma Swensson loved Handel's oratorio, *Messiah*, and decided that her Swedish neighbors should hear it, too. So she sent for the music, gathered a chorus of young people from the surrounding towns and farms, rehearsed them and let the welkin ring. That was in 1882.

Mrs. Swensson's sacred musical was such a success that it went on tour, in lumber wagons along dusty Kansas roads. . . . Next year they did it again. The chorus grew, acquired a permanent orchestra and conductor, hired famous soloists like

Lillian Nordica, Ernestine Schumann-Heink, Olive Fremstad. Lindsborg's annual *Messiah* became the biggest musical event in Kansas.

Howard W. Tuttle, in a two-column story on the festival in the March 26, 1939, issue of the *New York Times* wrote that in Lindsborg, the *Messiah* is religion—as much a part of the Swedish people's worship as the church services which they attend every Sunday.

It is an outpouring of the story they believe—the voice of John the Baptist crying in the wilderness; the birth of Jesus; His ministry; His crucifixion, and the triumphant resurrection with its resounding "Hallelujah". So when the Swedes sing their oratorio, it is more than a performance of musical quality. It has behind it a conviction of truth; of high purpose; of religious zeal that lifts its ecstasy to the sky and resounds in countless "Hallelujahs."

He wrote that Alma Swensson expected to take her place in the soprano section as she had every year.

But it was not to be. Alma did not sing in the 1939 presentation of *Messiah*. She had become ill after suffering a fall down the stairs in her home, and she did not have the strength to take her place in the chorus among her neighbors and friends—all those whom she had watched grow to maturity over her nearly sixty years in Lindsborg.

She just could not.

Celebrating Her Life

The Kansas Conference of the Augustana Synod, the Women's Missionary Society, Bethany College, and the people of Lindsborg came together to honor Alma on the occasion of her 78th birthday on December 11, 1937. Throughout the morning, college students serenaded her with songs and callers came to her door with greetings, well wishes, and gifts.

A program at Bethany Church had been organized by the Women's Missionary Society, perhaps realizing that their founder, influential leader, and friend was reaching a tender, precipitous age.

The festive program opened with an organ concert by Dr. Brasé. All 500 members in the audience then sang the hymn that had become a theme song for Alma's life: "What Shall I Render to My God for All His Gifts to Me":

> What shall I render to my God
> For all His gifts to me?
> Sing heaven and earth, rejoice, and praise His glorious majesty.
>
> O let me praise Thee while I live,
> And praise Thee when I die,
> And praise Thee when I rise again, and to eternity.
>
> Mysterious depths of endless love
> Our admiration raise;
> My God, Thy Name exalted is
> Above our highest praise.

Devotions and prayers were given by area clergy, then a host of greetings and telegrams were read from friends and colleagues around the country. Agnes Christianson, a missionary to India home on furlough, compared Alma to the biblical Phoebe—"a servant of the church and a friend to many." Willis Olson played a clarinet solo accompanied by his sister Ruth.

Mrs. F. O. Johnson, representing the synod board, recalled the times of her own childhood when she came to Lindsborg as a young girl. "Everything centered around Dr. and Mrs. Swensson," she said. "They were the leaders in all the activities in the church and in the college, and everything they undertook to do flourished." Mrs. Johnson described for the audience the old Bethany Church at that time with the organ on the front balcony, above the altar, where Alma sat as organist. "The choir sat to her right and a group of boys with horns to her left, and the music that they rendered under her leadership almost raised the roof." As Mrs. Johnson presented a gift to Alma on behalf of the synod Women's Missionary Society, the entire audience rose in tribute. Now it was Alma's turn to speak.

"I am overwhelmed, words fail me," Alma said. "This is entirely too much." She commented that throughout her life, in the darkest hours as well as the happiest, that Psalm 23 had been a source of joy. "Keeping busy has kept me in good health. There has been no time to sit around and brood."

Alma ended her remarks by describing the privilege of serving God through the Women's Missionary Society and the Bethany Oratorio Society, and she pleaded with all who heard her to carry on the work. In a gracious gesture, she paid a beautiful tribute to Anna Bergin, whose recent death in an auto accident shocked the church and community.

Then the Oratorio Society, gathered for her birthday celebration, sang two choruses from *Messiah*. Pastor J. E. Liljedahl of Salina pronounced the benediction upon all, and the entire congregation sang the Doxology, "Praise God From Whom All Blessings Flow." One can only imagine the effect of the congregational singing on all who were present. Following the program, refreshments were served in the church social rooms which were "artistically decorated." Alma, it was reported, stood surrounded by many floral bouquets.[132]

Alma posted a thank you in the Women's Missionary Society's *Missions-Tidning*. She underlined the words herself.

Dear Friends,

Words fail me in expressing my heartfelt appreciation and gratitude for the lovely birthday celebration prepared for me. I wish to thank you all for the monetary gifts, for all the beautiful flowers, tributes, and friendly greetings!

I feel entirely unworthy. If in a small way I have been able to serve, I am truly grateful!

Again I wish to thank you most sincerely for all kindness shown me—not only now, but throughout the years!

The good Lord bless you all!

Very sincerely yours in the Master's service,

Alma C. Swensson
(Mrs. Carl Swensson)

The new year, 1938, dawned, and Annie, in her thirty-first year as professor of Bethany College, now served as dean of women at Bethany College as well as head of the dramatics department. She often brought her students to their home for social occasions or after-play reviews, celebrations, and refreshments. Alma's twin grandchildren, Carl and Louise Vestling, now age twenty-five, came to visit, and Alma enjoyed their company and conversations.

It was in the autumn of 1938 Alma suffered a fall. She had gotten out of bed at night and came too close to the front stairway where she tumbled down the entire flight of stairs. The doctor was called, and he discovered that there were no broken bones, but difficult bruises. Her steps became measured, and her energy waned.

In early February 1939, a lovely eightieth birthday celebration was held in honor of Alma's longtime friend, Sarah Noyd Gröndal. But Alma is not listed among the guests who came to bring Sarah well wishes. Nor was she among those who attended a celebration for one of the oldest members of Bethany Church, John Lundstrom, who observed his ninety-second birthday with family, friends, and neighbors. And she was absent from the farewell surprise for Mr. and Mrs. Verner Olson, longtime community residents who were moving from Lindsborg to Cheyenne, Wyoming.[133]

By the late spring of 1939, Alma regained her strength to some degree. She and Annie hosted a wedding reception in their yard for Herman's daughter, Elinor Lind, who married Lee Gahnstrom on a beautiful, sunny June 5.

Later that spring, the Augustana Synod once again held its convention at Bethany Church, and her beloved Women's Missionary Society met at the same time. It was now thirty-five years after Carl's death; thirty-five years since they envisioned the expansion of the church for the 1904 Synod gathering, the work of the Palmquist Brothers, the placement of the jewel-like windows; the new organ—all of which Carl never lived to see.

At the beginning of their convention, the visiting Women's Missionary Society members from throughout the country explored Lindsborg with a good look around the community. "So this is Lindsborg," a new generation of Lutheran women proclaimed, "as we gathered from the East, West, North, and South. The Oberammergau of the Prairies, where the famous *Messiah* has been rendered for the fifty-sixth time! Lindsborg is the birthplace of the Women's Missionary Society, and the home of Bethany College!"[134]

The Women's Missionary Society convention schedule was filled with business proceedings, and Alma was able to be at most of the sessions, although her hearing was such that those who sat next to her had to share what was occurring at the meeting. [135] Alma's old friend, Emmy Evald, read her president's report as usual. Four missionaries on furlough spoke of their work in far-away places: Margaret Samuelson, "Witness to

The 1939 meeting of the Women's Missionary Society. Alma is seated fourth from the right in the front row. Emmy Evald is seated third from the left.

Africa"; Sister Elvira Person, "Witness in China"; Sister Astrid Erling, "In the Hsuchang Hospital During the War"; Miss Ethel Akins, "Revival in China."

The Young Women's Missionary Society, which Alma helped nurture all through her active life, reported on the desks they had purchased for the girls school in Africa. And the Women's Missionary Society sent $500 for a dispensary at Mutinka, Africa. Three young women were commissioned for mission service—all of them named Margaret: Margaret Hawkinson, an educational missionary to India; Margaret Friberg, an evangelistic missionary to China; Margaret Peterson, R.N., a medical missionary to Africa. Margaret Hawkinson and Margaret Peterson both grew up in Kansas, both were alumnae of Bethany College, both had sung in the Bethany Oratorio Society as students, both had studied elocution with Annie Swensson and had been guests in Alma's home.

One afternoon, the convention walked en masse to the spot where the Bethany parsonage stood in 1892, Carl and Alma's home. Present among the delegates and visitors to the convention were six of the charter members—Dr. Emmy Evald, Mrs. F. O. Johnson, Mrs. John Welin, Mrs. Luther Swensson, Mrs. Eric Leksell, and Alma Swensson who had welcomed those fifty women to that organizing meeting, filled with the fire of mission and the support of men like Carl who spoke on their behalf on the convention floor. The Women's Missionary Society held a brief memorial service "on the memorable site," and a photo was taken. Alma is there, seated in the front row, wearing a black dress, her legs crossed at the ankles, her hands folded neatly on her lap, a brooch at her neck, her serene face crowned with white hair. All the women are looking into the Kansas sunshine. The women decided to erect a memorial tablet at the historic site.[136] Alma's friends later commented that she appeared especially happy and joyous that day.[137] The local newspapers reported that "the Kansas women were most cordial." Alma's sense of hospitality had endured, and the whole community was suffused with the importance of extending a gracious welcome to guests of church, campus, and home. The Women's Missionary Society pioneers would not be together again.

Alma published her last issue as editor for the society that gave her such purpose when she was searching for an expression of herself.

Later in the summer, Professor Birger Sandzén received national recognition when his woodcut, "Blue Valley Farm," was included in the New York World's Fair Gallery of American Art Today. Kansas farmers harvested the wheat crop that averaged a rather modest twelve bushels to the acre.

The days grew shorter, and it was time for Armistice Day. Many members of the Oratorio Society recalled the vision before them of those 8,000 soldiers in their khaki uniforms at Camp Funston in 1918, for whom the Oratorio Society sang *Messiah* twice on the same spring day. Two weeks later, the Americans celebrated Thanksgiving Day on November 23. And on November 30, the renowned Swedish tenor, Jussi Björling, almost a hometown boy, sang in concert at Presser Hall and was crowned "King of Tenors."[138] Choirs throughout the countryside were rehearsing anthems for Advent and Christmas.

On Saturday, December 9, the day before the Second Sunday in Advent, Annie was in the midst of preparations for a surprise party to honor her mother on her eightieth birthday. Annie had decorated their home for the festivities, the table was set, and everything ready for a most happy celebration. But hours before the guests arrived, Alma suffered a stroke and drifted into a coma. Bertha was called home. Just at sunset on Saturday, December 16, Alma breathed her last. Her daughters remembered that the Bethany Church bell was ringing in the sabbath.

Funeral services for Alma Christina Lind Swensson were held Tuesday, December 19, at Presser Hall Auditorium. Her body lay in state in Presser Hall for two hours as hundreds passed by to pay their deep respects. She was enrobed in her wedding dress, the dress she had worn fifty-nine years earlier when she became Carl's life companion.[139] The Bethany Orchestra played the "Pastoral Symphony" from *Messiah* as her casket was carried to the front of the auditorium. If one did not know its origins the sweet, gentle, lilting, and soft strains of the "Pastoral" could have easily been an interpretation of the Kansas landscape. Floral tributes from throughout the country were arranged on the Presser Hall stage as her casket is placed on the catafalque. The Bethany Oratorio Society opened the service by singing "Surely He Hath Borne Our Griefs." Scripture reading and prayer were given by Pastor N. E. Olsson. Marie Seeliger, a gifted Bethany College vocal student, sang "I Know That My Redeemer Liveth." Alma's good and gracious friend, Ernst Pihlblad, now sixty-six years of age and still serving as president of Bethany College, preached the sermon. The text chosen for the occasion was one she recited each day, Psalm 121: "I will lift up mine eyes unto the mountains, from whence shall my help come." In his sermon, Dr. Pihlblad said,

> Mrs. Swensson had a spirit of hopeful optimism. She never confessed to defeat, but hope lived in her heart throughout all. Her hopefulness, which throughout all the years, has been one of her characteristic traits, was not a superficial attitude which we are prone to adopt, that everything will turn out all right. It was a faith which had found its expression in the assurance of the Psalmist of old.[140]

Dr. Bergin pronounced the benediction, and the oratorio society concluded with the resounding "Worthy Is the Lamb." When the last great and thankful Amen was sung, the congregation rose as the casket was carried in procession out of Presser Hall, down the steps to the waiting hearse. Oak leaves, still clinging to their branches, rustled in the breeze. Cottonwood trees, planted so many years earlier, stood like sentinels along the campus path as the procession made its way down the walk. A handful of pine trees caught the Kansas wind. And remnants of buffalo grass wavered as a reminder of those early pioneer days when Alma first stepped off the train onto the Kansas prairie. Old and dear friends served as pallbearers—Dr. H. G. Johnson, Lennard Gunnerson, Thure Jaderborg, Oscar Lofgren, Emory Lindquist, and Oscar Thorsen—accompanying her body along the mile-long dusty road to Elmwood Cemetery. A quartette sang at her grave as the sun set on the cold, windy, wintry December day. Alma Christina Lind Swensson was laid to rest in a grave next to her husband, Carl. Her journey was complete.

Six days later, the brass ensemble in the bell tower of Bethany Church announced the dawning of Christmas morning. During *Julotta* the Bethany Church Choir and congregation remembered Alma as they sang the Christmas hymns and anthems they held in their hearts, the music that connected them to all the generations before.

A few weeks after Christmas and the turn of the year to 1940, rehearsals began again for Handel's *Messiah*. Emory K. Lindquist, now acting president of Bethany College, stood before the oratorio society of more than 500 people—high school students, college students, representatives of the third and fourth generations of singers, sitting side by side by side each other at the first rehearsal of the season. Dr. Brasé, standing off the podium, his baton in hand, listened and nodded as Dr. Lindquist told the chorus that their work was "keeping faith with the past." His words took on added meaning because of Alma's death. "Her death has meant the end of an era in the organization's history," Dr. Lindquist said. People remembered Alma and the music that not only brought them together but made them a rare community. Then Dr. Brasé stepped on to the podium and the chorus sang in tribute "Behold the Lamb of God," memorializing also Mrs. Hjalmer Wetterstrom, the oratorio society's faithful secretary and member for many years, and Francis Plym, a benefactor of the college who had also died within the year.[141]

The Measure of Her Gift

The measure of Alma Christina Lind Swensson's gift to community, college, and church touches generations yet today. During her fifty-nine years in Lindsborg, Alma created a culture of leadership, service, and music that transcends time. When she stepped off the train on that late September day in 1880, the people of Lindsborg were just ten years from settlement. Alma was a representative of frontier women who did not reject the fact that her life journey brought her to a small town on the Great Plains. She was a force for overcoming the conditions all were going through together, and she brought along with her all who wanted to be part of the effort in making their community a place of beauty and culture.[142]

The church brought them together first for common interests and purpose, for a familiar and safe language in a strange landscape, and for the comfort found in singing hymns they had known since childhood.

Rehearsing Handel's *Messiah* under Alma's leadership brought a broader community together. This is where they learned the diction and pronunciation of the language of their new land. In essence, it could be said that Alma Lind Swensson gave the immigrants their American voice. And she also gave them the sense and appreciation for the harmonies and forms of classical music.

People wonder at this today. How did Alma teach them this major, world-renowned oratorio when no one except she and Carl had ever heard the music?

To discover the answer to that question, it is important to remember that the Swedish people have lived the culture of singing since the Lutheran Reformation came to Sweden in 1529. Hymns after the Reformation were written in the vernacular of the people. An official hymnal or *Psalmbok* was published in 1695 and used for more than 125 years. The second official hymnal, published in 1819, was used for 118 years and became a national treasure of the Swedish people. It is the book that immigrants packed in their America trunks as one of their most cherished possessions.[143] This 1819 *Psalmbok* was brought by those who came to Kansas with Olof Olsson and was used both as a devotional book in their new prairie homes and at worship services in that first little church of sod and stone. And Olsson prepared the first choir to sing a selection from that *Psalmbok* on New Year's Day, 1870. The Lindsborg people were singing people.

While they had not heard Handel's great oratorio, for it was music generally heard by those who lived in large cities, the sounds would be familiar to their ears and to their sensibilities as Alma played parts of *Messiah* for them on her piano in the parsonage.

Choral conductor Sigrid Johnson,[144] renowned for her special skill at blending voices, perfecting tone and assisting with vocal production—both psychologically and physiologically—has said that because Handel's music is tonal, it is a clean harmonic sound, easily put in their ears, hearts, and souls. The music has a familiar pattern, and the resolutions come to a conclusion they would understand," Johnson explains. "They would not have to re-learn how to use their voices for this music. The music made sense to their ears, and it could easily become part of them based on what they already could feel as singers."

Alma would have taught them the music note by note, phrase by phrase, line by line. Sectional rehearsals—those of sopranos, altos, tenors, and basses—were critical to learning the score. "Alma might have found a leader in each section who could take them to another room in the church or parsonage and work on their specific parts while she worked with another section," Johnson says. She continues:

> The critical thing in training a choir is helping the choir get the music in their psyche, in their conscience, by using imagery to help them achieve what she would like them to achieve. She might liken a certain phrase to an ethereal cloud or certainly to sheep in a pasture on a neighbor's farm for the chorus, "All We Like Sheep." The conductor had to know what she wanted where, and how to explain that to her choir so that it would make sense to them. Then she had to help them relax—to not be tense—and to enjoy the music. She knew what the voice

felt like because she was also a singer. Not all conductors are singers.

Johnson goes on to explain that there are two different temperaments of conductors. "There is the educating conductor who takes a choir from the beginning stages of learning the piece and prepares the singers for performance. That process is step-by-step, note-by-note in rehearsals and practice. There is also the performing conductor who leads the choir in a performance before an audience. For the educating conductor, all the magic happens in the training."

The general consensus is that Alma was an educating conductor who had the ability and found enjoyment in preparing and familiarizing her choir with a piece of music from the first time they opened the score until they walked onto the performance stage.

Alma, though she had prepared the choir, did not conduct the choir at the first performance of *Messiah* in 1882. Joseph Osborn, who had conducted the oratorio at Augustana College came from Rock Island with an orchestra, and Olof Olsson was the organist. Alma sang the soprano solos of *Messiah*. But the obituary read at her funeral by Bethany College President Ernst Pihlblad, who had known her for more than fifty years, stated, "Mrs. Swensson trained the organization and acted as soloist at its first public appearance in the spring of 1882. This was in a day and age when public sentiment did not countenance a woman acting as a choir leader; as a result, a man leader was brought in for the concerts."[145] Whether that was a sentiment suggested by her more liberated daughters as they consulted with Dr. Pihlblad while planning their mother's funeral or whether Alma was happy to give the baton to Joseph Osborn and be the soprano soloist will not be known.

Sigrid Johnson suggests that it may not have been a gender issue. "Women as composers and performers were coming into their own in the nineteenth century—Clara Schumann (1819 to 1896), Fanny Mendelssohn (1805 to 1847), Amy Marcy Beach (1867 to 1944), Nina Hagerup Grieg (1845 to 1935), and Sweden's own Jenny Lind (1820 to 1887) who was a household name before her U.S. concert tour in 1850."

Singing *Messiah* may have provided another benefit for the Scandinavian Lutherans who often are characterized by the tendency for quiet expression, of minimalist emotion. Historian Sandra L. Myres explains that when an immigrant would speak of, for example, "a pleasant view," he or she might describe a quiet river valley, a spectacular sunset, or a broad vista of snow-capped mountains.[146] Imagine, then, how Handel's music allowed the Swedish immigrants of Lindsborg to express a pent-up joy, an outburst of emotion in the "Hallelujah" chorus, for example, or the resounding opening chords of "Worthy Is the Lamb." The music of *Messiah* allowed them to express emotions in a way they would otherwise not have known in their experience.

Alma served as a role model to young women in a small prairie town who sought a path to follow their calling. Alma Luise Olson, for example, born near Lindsborg in 1884 and a graduate of Bethany College, became a correspondent for the *New York Times* in the Scandinavian countries for seventeen years prior to the outbreak of World War II. Olson's comprehensive study of basic politics in Scandinavia was published by Lippincott in 1940 under the title *Scandinavia: The Background for Neutrality.* She was an expert linguist, internationalist, and supporter of the United Nations. Shortly after the publication of her book, which was recognized as the authoritative work in the field, she became the first American to receive Sweden's highest award, the Vasa Medallion.

Ebba Sundstrom, born on a farm near Lindsborg in 1896, became the first American-born woman to conduct a symphony orchestra when she was named conductor of the Chicago Woman's Symphony Orchestra. By 1935, she was in her sixth season as conductor when *Time* magazine wrote about her and the orchestra in an article "Music: Women on Their Own."

> Men were hired to blow the difficult wind instruments at first but now all 80 players are women and for six years the conductor has been graceful, blonde Ebba Sundstrom, who is determined that the orchestra shall sound professional. Conductor Sundstrom has worked at music since she was a child on a farm in Lindsborg, Kans. At 7 she played the violin, at 13 she organized a trio, played in hotels and theatres.

> Conductor Sundstrom, practical about her job, says: Women's orchestras must not merely play well; they must strive to play better than the orchestras if they are going to be successful.[147]

The following summer, the *Chicago Tribune* wrote about the influence of Ebba's hometown:

It was to Lindsborg, small community of high artistic aspirations, that her grandparents immigrated, establishing the family on a farm. Ebba was the youngest of seven children—three sons, four daughters.

Bethany College was the center about which Lindsborg's deepest interest revolved. From it sprang the Bethany Oratorio Society that, with its Messiah Festivals, won for the prairie settlement a place in the musical sun.

The great of the musical world had discovered Lindsborg. And thither they came, the Metropolitan's darlings, to fraternize with the prairie singers. Small Ebba thrilled to her town's legend of brothers De Reszke—Jean, whose genius an older generation held, surpassed Caruso's; Edouard, the baritone, almost as great an artist. "Beauteous Nordica was the first whom Ebba heard. . . . To this point every important element in her life was one to encourage the child artist in her ambitions."

One must certainly consider Alma's influence in service to the church. First, as co-organizer of the Augustana Women's Missionary Society, and editor of *Missions-Tidnings,* she put the idea of service to the church before 25,000 household subscribers, helping influence young women who felt called to serve the church in far-away places. An example are the three young women, all with the name of Margaret, who felt called to mission work, and were commissioned as missionaries on the same day in Lindsborg at the Women's Missionary Society meeting, June 16, 1939. Margaret Peterson served on the mission field for more than thirty years in Tanzania; Margaret Hawkinson Coleman was a missionary in India for forty-four years; and Margaret Friberg in China, then Africa, for a total of forty-three years. And Alma, through her paper, helped families, especially women and children, understand the ethic of collaboration. The pennies, nickels, and dimes they saved in little cardboard boxes could help build a children's hospital in India or purchase books and desks for schools in Africa. In 1998, sixty-two women published their missionary experiences in a collaborative book, *Touched By the African Soul.*[148] At least fifteen of the authors were young girls, including Margaret Peterson, when Alma was editor of *Missions-Tidning*.

Doris Hedeen Spong became involved in the work of the Women's Missionary Society while still in high school. In 1926, at the age of sixteen, she was elected the Young Women's Missionary Society secretary. She deeply believed in the equality of women in the church and was an early champion for the ordination of women. Doris, who was both organist and choir director for congregations in Texas, Illinois, Nebraska, Minnesota, and Kansas, also served the national church as president of the Augustana Women's Missionary Society, and then president of the Lutheran Church Women of the Lutheran Church in America.[149]

The yard around the parsonage where Alma and Carl made their home more than 100 years ago—where they welcomed guests and raised their intelligent, gifted, and beautiful daughters, Bertha and Annie, where they watched young women in dresses of white lawn pick bouquets from a nearby field of daisies, who may have been humming tunes they learned from Alma in choir—is now the scene of many Lindsborg community celebrations. The parsonage was moved away in the late 1920s, and in its footprint a pond with a fountain was created. The parsonage yard is now known as Swensson Park.

At *Midsommar*, under tall cottonwood and elm trees, Swensson Park is filled with children—young boys in vests and knickers of blue, yellow, black, and red with woven braids flying at the tops of their long white socks. Little girls have wreaths of flowers in their hair and are wearing Swedish costumes—jumpers in shades of yellow, red, and that certain Swedish blue with crisp white blouses, cuffs and collars edged with tatted lace; tied at the waist are freshly ironed flowered aprons or aprons with woven stripes that give a homespun look. Their black shoes and white tights complete a postcard photograph that could be sent from Sunnemo, Broddarp, Stockholm, Uppsala, Härnösand, or Mora. But this is Kansas, and the girls and boys are re-enacting a time and grace from their great-great grandmothers' old country—great-great-grandmothers who had said good-bye to these customs in Sweden 140 years earlier, and made new homes on this flat valley on the Great Plains.

At Bethany Church—the big white church with the tall steeple across the park, the place where Alma and her husband Pastor Carl Aaron Swensson together created a culture of respectful Lutheran worship and liturgy—children grow up singing anthems that remain with them for the rest of their lives.

Bethany Church is also the place of the annual Saint Lucia celebration. On the Saturday nearest December 13, a Saint Lucia program is presented by nine year olds in the morning and by teenagers in the afternoon, members of the Swedish High School Folkdancers. Proudly, and gladly they sing the same songs that children in Sweden are singing on Saint Lucia Day. The tender, sweet young voices sing the carefully rehearsed music and lyrics:

> *Nu tändas tusen juleljus på jordens mörka rund.*
> *Och tusen, tusen stråla ock på himlens djupblå grund.*

> A thousand Christmas candles now
> Are lit upon the earth,
> A thousand more in heaven glow
> To honor Jesus' birth.

The legend of Saint Lucia is read, and then a nine-year-old girl at the end of the morning pageant, and an eighteen-year-old girl at the afternoon's pageant will wear the crown of candles while her classmates sing in soft, gentle voices:

> *Natten går tunga fjät runt gård och stuva.*
> *Kring jord som sol'n förlät, skuggorna ruva.*
> *Då i vårt mörka hus stiger med tända ljus*
> *Sankta Lucia, Sankta Lucia, Sankta Lucia*

> The night walks with heavy steps 'round farm and cottage.
> Around the earth, forsaken by the sun, shadows are brooding.
> Then into our dark house steps with lighted candles
> Saint Lucia, Saint Lucia, Saint Lucia.

During the singing of this song, the Lindsborg Saint Lucia, dressed in a robe of white tied with a crimson sash and bravely wearing the crown of lighted candles, serves coffee and *pepparkakor*[150] to her family members

Julotta, December 25, 1999, at Bethany Lutheran Church, Lindsborg, Kansas.

who are seated in the front row. Soon, after tears are dried on many faces, the audience will be refreshed with traditional coffee fare for this festive, special day.

In the darkest early morning hours of December 25, brass musicians gather in the bell tower of the big white church, fling open the doors, and signal with their music in the clear, cool, early Kansas morning that the *Julotta* is about to begin. Their bright sounds are heard all through the town. The sanctuary of Bethany Church is filled to capacity. Candelabra, made more than a half century ago by a local ironworker from a Swedish design, tower above the congregation and brightly burn with red candles. Additional candelabra are placed on the deep windowsills of the stone church and, like votives, are lit before the vibrant stained glass windows installed in 1904 in memory of Swedish immigrant families:

"*Till minne af Olof och Brita Olsson.*"
"*Till minne af Peter och Maria Pearson.*"
"*Till minne af Maria Lisa Olsson*"[151]

While *Julotta* has been conducted in English since the 1920s, the congregation still sings two signature hymns in Swedish:

När juldags morgon gilmmar,
Jag vill till stallet gå,
Der Gud i nattens timmar
Re'n hvilar uppå strå.
Der Gud i nattens timmar
Re'n hvilar uppå strå.

When Christmas morn is dawning,
In faith I would repair
Unto the lowly manger;
My Savior lieth there,
Unto the lowly manger;
My Savior lieth there.

Var hälsad, sköna morgonstund, som av profeters helga mun
är oss bebådad vorden!
Du stora dag du sälla dag, på vilken himlens väl behag
änu besöker jorden!
Unga, sjunga,
med de gamla, sig församla jordens böner
kring den störste av dess söner.

All hail to thee, O blessed morn!
To tidings long by prophets borne
Has thou fulfillment given.
O sacred and immortal day, when unto earth, in glorious ray,
Descends the grace of heaven!
Singing, ringing,
Sounds are blending,
Praises sending
Unto heaven
For the Savior to us given.

These are the very same hymns sung long ago during *Julotta* at Broddarp, Sunnemo, Uppsala, Andover, Moline, and, since 1869 at Lindsborg. It is the great gift of music that bridges generations and distances, that helps time stand still, that touches one's heart with those who are far away both in time and thought.

While Lindsborg clearly celebrates and embraces Swedish heritage, there have always been ties to contemporary Swedish culture, nurtured by both Carl and Alma, as Carl recruited teachers from Sweden's prestigious universities. There are student exchanges with Sweden through Mora *Folkhogskola*, the *Sigtunaskolan Humanistiska Läroverket*, and most recently, at Karlstad University in Värmland when current Bethany College President Edward Leonard and Karlstad University's Professor Thomas A. Wennstam established an exchange agreement in January 2011. The agreement received the blessing of Bishop Esbjörn Hagberg of the Karlstad Diocese. "It is so important to meet, learn from each other, and build relations between institutions and people. To build bridges to history is to build bridges of peace!" Bishop Hagberg said.

An enriching program for Bethany College and Lindsborg in the twenty-first century is the Pearson Distinguished Professor of Swedish Studies Program, an endowed fund created by the late Gerald "Bud" Pearson that allows distinguished Swedes to spend a semester on campus and in the community each year. Pearson developed the program in 1998 so "that present-day Swedish culture and experience can illuminate and strengthen life in the United States." The Pearson Distinguished Professors include Eskil Hemberg, director of the Royal Swedish Opera; Beate Sydhoff, secretary general of the Royal Academy of Fine Art; Håkan Hagegård, internationally renowned opera star; poet and novelist Ylva Eggehorn; journalist Arne Ruth; theologians Dr. Krister Stendahl, Dr. Hans Ucko, and Dr. Kjell Ove Nilsson; environmental educator Jimmy Sjöblom; anthropologist Dr. Brita Stendahl; forensic scientist Dr. Peter Savolainen; composer Per Harling; artist Jordi Arkö.

Just as the twentieth anniversary of Bethany College was a great cause for celebration in 1901, the 125th anniversary provided an opportunity for celebrating both the accomplishments of the college and a look to the future. With a grant from the Marcus och Amalia Wallenberg Foundation of Stockholm, the Pearson Distinguished Professors of Swedish Studies flew to Lindsborg to discuss issues of the future with American counterparts during a symposium, "Images Across the Sea: Sweden and American 2025." The Swedes and Americans discussed media, literature, museums, sustainability, theology, and music. Vocal ensembles of the community performed a concert celebrating contemporary Swedish and American composers. The three-day event closed with a gala candlelit dinner held in the Swedish Pavilion from the 1904 World's Fair. Later in the academic year, internationally renowned baritone Håkan Hagegård brought four of the finest young operatic voices from the Royal Swedish Academy to Lindsborg. The soloists, Mia Karlsson, Ivonne Fuchs, Martin Vanaberg, Andreas Lundmark, with Hagegärd presented a recital during the festival and performed the solos for *Messiah* and J. S. Bach's *Passion of Our Lord According to Saint Matthew.*[152]

It is Palm Sunday 2005. The Honorable Jan Eliasson, Swedish ambassador to the United States and world diplomat, is seated in the front row of the balcony in Presser Hall Auditorium next to Bethany College President Paul Formo and his wife, Pat. Jan Eliasson has just been elected president of the United Nations General Assembly and is in Lindsborg to pay tribute to the Bethany Oratorio Society and Bethany College on its 125th Anniversary. Earlier in the day he unveiled a monument on campus inscribed with the words of another Swedish diplomat, the late Dag Hammarskjöld, secretary general of the United Nations: For all that has been, thanks. For all that is to come, yes.[153]

At 3:00 p.m., Daniel Mahraun, conductor of the Oratorio Society, walks briskly on stage, then steps on the podium. He turns to the audience, and with a wave of his baton, gestures to the balcony. "Ladies and gentlemen," he announces, "Ambassador Jan Eliasson of Sweden." His Excellency rises to acknowledge the loud and prolonged applause from the audience, singers, and orchestra. After the applause, the ambassador is seated. Mahraun turns to the performers and gives the downbeat to begin the performance of *Messiah*, an echo of what Alma began more than a century ago. The delicate strains of "Pastoral Symphony" fill the air.

Outside of Presser Hall on this day, flowering redbud, pear, and cherry trees add visions of lace under the broad, bright, blue Kansas sky. The winter wheat crop is a breathtaking carpet of green on the surrounding farm fields. After summer's wheat harvest, wild sunflowers will stand in tall array along the roadways. Soon, a new generation of Bethany College students will begin their studies. Soon enough the candles will be lit on the crown of Saint Lucia and the brass ensemble in the bell tower will call worshippers to *Julotta*. Shortly after New Year's Day, the Oratorio Society will begin rehearsals for *Messiah*. The miracle of Easter is heard again. Across all the seasons of the year, Alma's legacy renews the spirit. With grace, she helped transform a frontier community through the power of hospitality and singing, creating a place where music, art, and history thrive. She lived her life with certain faith.

Alma's epic life journey is part of the magnificent narrative of American stories and a ribbon in the intricate tapestry of women's achievement.

Acknowledgments

Finding the threads of Alma Lind Swensson's life and weaving them together has brought a good deal of joy to my own life. And with that, I have a great deal of gratitude to a host of people who helped find the pieces, who made the research possible, who encouraged my research, who said, "Yes! Alma's story must be told." My heartfelt thanks to:

Charlotte Ternstrom, archivist of Bethany Lutheran Church; Denise Carson, librarian and archivist at Bethany College; Jennifer Gahnstrom, Alma's great-grand niece, whose shared Lind family materials that were priceless; Pastor Noni Strand; Jayne Norlin; Mark and Joyce Peterson; Margaret Eddy; Jane Brunsell; Jim and Donna Ruble; Jim Turner; Becky Anderson; Lenora Lynam; all of Lindsborg; and Alf and Maud Brorson of both Lindsborg and Torsby, Sweden, whose history of Olof and Anna Olsson is inspiring.

Heartfelt thanks to Judy Calcote, Jamie Hoehn, and Debbie Miller—my immensely helpful colleagues at the Minnesota Historical Society; to Sigrid Johnson of St. Olaf College; Jack Swanson and Mim Manfred of Normandale Lutheran Church in Edina; Marlys Peterson of First Lutheran Church in St. Paul; Suzanne Blue, Rhoda Gilman, Jeri Reilly, Ann Thorson Walton, Mike Edwins, Kurt Meyer.

My gratitude to Ed and Patty Lindell, Bruce Karstadt, Katherine Hanson, and Kathleen Segerhammer Hurty who read an early draft, gave helpful suggestions, and said, "Yes, continue."

Many, many, many thanks to Lilly Setterdahl, Chuck Holmgren, and Jan Johnson (and our God moment) at First Lutheran Church in Moline, Illinois; to Janet Meyer and Kathleen Seusy at the Rock Island County Historical Society; to Jill Seaholm and Susanne Titus at the Swenson Swedish Immigration Center, to Special Collections Librarian Jamie

Nelson at Augustana College, Rock Island; to the Hurtys for allowing Chuck and me to stay in their apartment; to Joel Thoreson ELCA reference archivist.

To my husband, Chuck, for his exceptional patience, insight, and encouragement in this project, and for our journey together. I am very grateful, and I love him so much. To our children, Karna and Kirk, for their interest.

This is also an opportunity to give thanks for the memory of Dr. Emeroy Johnson, the pastor who baptized and confirmed me at Scandian Grove Lutheran Church, Norseland, Minnesota, and to his daughter Grace Johnson Karstad. Dr. Johnson first kindled my interest in church and local history. Grace taught me to love the music of the church.

Endnotes

1   https://broddarp.se.

2   http://wadbring.com/historia/undersidor/broddarp.htm.

3   Several sources say that Alma was born in Bredaryd, but this is an error, likely due to a handwriting issue. The handwritten source was found shortly after Alma's death in 1939, in the papers of Ernst Pihlblad who wrote the obituary for the church and other publications. Lind family papers from Andover, Illinois, signed by Pastor Jonas Swensson, clearly show that Alma was born at Broddarp.

4   Hos Gubben Lind, *En Besök hos en Svensk-American av Gamla Stammen* (A Visit with a Swedish-American of Old Lineage) (Ungdomsvännen: Maj 1903); trans. Emory Lindquist (Rock Island: June 1979).

5   Swedish State Church Records, Broddarp Parish.

6   June Drennings Holmquist, ed, *They Chose Minnesota* (St. Paul: Minnesota Historical Society Press, 1981).

7   H. Arnold Barton, ed, *Letters from the Promised Land* (Minneapolis: University of Minnesota Press, 1975).

8   See translation by O.V. Anderson of *Rågra råd och underrättelfer för Utvandrare till Amerifas Förenta Stater af Erl Carlsson.* Appendix in Emory Lindquist, *Shepherd of an Immigrant People: The Story of Erland Carlsson* (Rock Island: Augustana Historical Society, 1978).

9   *Praying Together for 150 Years: Anniversary History of Augustana Evangelical Lutheran Church: Pastor Lynn Bergren* (Andover: Augustana Evangelical Lutheran Church, 2000).

10 Swensson was ordained October 8, 1851, in the cathedral at Växjö.

11 *Julotta* was transplanted to America by immigrants from Sweden and is a fond remembrance of many generations of Swedish-Americans. Bethany Lutheran Church celebrates *Julotta* at 6:00 a.m., just as it has since 1870. Although the service is now in English, the two hymns mentioned here are sung in Swedish.

12 Esbjorn was the founder of the church at Andover, also in 1850.

13 Lilly Setterdahl, *Swedes in Moline, Illinois: 1847-2002* (2003).

14 Minutes of First Lutheran Church, Moline, Illinois. The name was changed from Svenska Evangeliska Lutherska Församlingen (Swedish Evangelical Lutheran Church) to First Lutheran Church in the 1920s.

15 First Lutheran Church records, Moline, Illinois.

16 Kathleen Seusy, Diann Moore, Curtis C. Roseman, Regena Schantz, *Echoes From Riverside Cemetery, Moline, Illinois* (Moline: Heritage Documentaries, Inc., 2009).

17 Rock Island *Review*, May 28, 1875.

18 Ronald B. Bagnall, "The Augustana Liturgy—Part 3: An Extraordinary Ordinary," *The Augustana Heritage Newsletter*, Volume 7, Number 4 (Fall 2010).

19 Arnold J. Hultgren, "The Augustana Liturgy: Its Significance for Shaping a Community of Faith," *Lutheran Quarterly*, Volume XXIV.

20 "Holy, holy, holy is the Lord of hosts. The whole world is full of his glory."

21 Author interview with Dr. Jack Swanson, organist and scholar of the Augustana Lutheran Synod, Normandale Lutheran Church, Edina, Minnesota (January 2011).

22 Minutes of First Lutheran Church, Moline, Illinois, January 1, 1876. Alma received $100.00 and one offering from the Easter Mass.

23 Kathleen Seusy, Diann Moore, Curtis C. Roseman, Regena Schantz, *Echoes From Riverside Cemetery: Moline, Illinois* (Moline: Heritage Documentaries, Inc., 2009).

24 Rock Island *Daily Union* (May 3, 1878).

25 Rock Island *Daily Union* (May 25, 1878).

26 Anna Olsson's memoir, *En Prärieunges Funderingar* (A Prairie Child's Thoughts), was first published in Swedish in 1917, then translated by Martha Winblad and published by Bethany College in 1978, Elizabeth Jaderborg, ed. In 1927, Augustana Book Concern, Rock Island, published a Swedish-American dialect under the title, "I'm scairt."

27 A contemporary explanation of the Kansas climate is this, told to the author by a longtime Lindsborg area farmer: "You know, when God created the heavens and the earth, and it rained for forty days and forty nights? Well, Kansas got a quarter of an inch."

28 Värmland is the home of such writers and poets as Selma Lagerlöf, Gustaf Fröding, Esaias Tegnér, and Nils Ferlin, who based their writing on the story-telling tradition and local legend of the province.

29 Emory Lindquist, *Vision for a Valley: Olof Olsson and the Early History of Lindsborg* (Rock Island: Augustana Historical Society Press, 1970).

30 Ibid.

31 Sunnemo Pastor Monika Drewes preached on this theme in her sermon on Ascension Day (Kristi Himmelfördag), May 29, 2003.

32 Alf Brorson, *Mrs. Olof Olsson: the Story of Anna Lisa Jonsdotter and her Swedish-American Family* (Torsby: A-Ö Handelsbolag, 1998).

33 Ibid.

34   Emory Lindquist, *Vision for a Valley: Olof Olsson and the Early Hstory of Lindsborg* (Rock Island: Augustana Historical Society Press, 1970).

35   Ernst William Olson, L.H.D., *Olof Olsson: The Man, His Work, and His Thought* (Rock Island: Augustana Book Concern, 1941).

36   The table still exists in the sacristy of Bethany Lutheran Church, Lindsborg, Kansas.

37   Emory Lindquist, *Vision for a Valley: Olof Olsson and the Early Hstory of Lindsborg* (Rock Island: Augustana Historical Society Press, 1970).

38   Ernst William Olson, L.H.D., *Olof Olsson: The Man, His Work and His Thought* (Rock Island: Augustana Book Concern, 1941).

39   *Songs of the Homeland*, the Swedish hymnal beloved by generations. A plaque on the same Estey reed organ, now on display in the Martin Luther Room, Bethany Lutheran Church, Lindsborg, Kansas reads: "The first organ of the Ev Luth Bethany Church, Lindsborg, Kans. At the first service, Dr. Olsson played and sang Heml. Sang 285."

40   Edith Messenger Houghton, *Bethany Lutheran Church 125th Anniversary: God's Word Alive Forever* (Lindsborg: Bethany Lutheran Church, 1993).

41   Emory Lindquist, *Smoky Valley People* (Rock Island: Augustana Book Concern, 1953).

42   Anna Olsson, *A Child of the Prairie*. A translation from the Swedish of "*En Präieunges Funderingar,*" Martha Winblad, trans., Elizabeth Jaderborg, ed. (1978).

43   Emory Lindquist, *Bethany in Kansas: The History of a College* (Lindsborg: Bethany College Publications, 1975).

44   Emory Lindquist, *Smoky Valley People* (Rock Island: Augustana Book Concern, 1953).

45   Ibid.

46   Lindsborg *Localist* (August 16, 1879).

47   Ernst F. Pihlblad article, "Bethany College in Pioneer Swedish Culture in Central Kansas."

48   Lindsborg *Localist* (July 15, 1880).

49   Rock Island *Daily Union* (Thursday, September 16, 1880).

50   Original poem, written in Swedish, Lilly Setterdahl, trans. In 2011. Bethany College Archives.

51   Elizabeth Jaderborgm, "Swedish Architectural Influence in the Kansas Smoky Valley Community," *The Swedish Pioneer Historical Quarterly* (January 1981).

52   Emory Lindquist, *Bethany In Kansas: The History of a College* (Lindsborg: Bethany College, 1975).

53   Iola Register (April 12, 1901).

54   Born on a farm near West Salem, Wisconsin on September 14, 1860, Garland advocated that writers use "local color," using "such quality of texture and back-

ground that it could not have been written in any other place." Garland won the 1922 Pulitzer Prize for *A Daughter of the Middle Border.*

55 Nora Lind may have been Alma's sister; she would have been thirteen-years-old.

56 Emory Lindquist, *Bethany in Kansas: the History of a College* (Lindsborg: Bethany College, 1975).

57 *Saline County Journal* (July 1881).

58 Lindsborg *Localist* (December 29, 1881)

59 Lindquist, *Bethany in Kansas.* The Bethany Academy, founded in the sacristy of Bethany Church in 1881, was officially designated Bethany College in 1889.

60 Statistic from the Yale Alumni Weekly as reported in *Bethany Magazine* (November 1902).

61 The reference is to Joshua Hasselquist, Swensson's classmate in Augustana's first graduating class.

62 Ernst William Olson, L.H.D., *Olof Olsson: The Man, His Work, and His Thought* (Rock Island: Augustana Book Concern, 1941).

63 Emory Lindquist, *Bethany in Kansas: The History of a College* (Lindsborg: Bethany College, 1975).

64 Anna Swensson may have been the younger sister of Carl Swensson. She would have been nineteen at the time. Backman and Linder were soloists at the performance in Rock Island.

65 Edward Nelander, the first president of Bethany College, resigned in 1889 to take a pastorate at the Swedish Lutheran Church in Kansas City, Missouri. The Bethany College board appointed Carl the second president of the college.

66 Author interview on April 3, 2010, with Margaret Eddy, granddaughter of Bror and Sarah Noyd Gröndal.

67 Emory Lindquist, *G.N. Malm: A Swedish Immigrant's Varied Career* (Lindsborg: Smoky Valley Historical Association, 1989).

68 Birger Sandzén article in "The Smoky Valley in the After Years," by Ruth Bergin Billdt and Elizabeth Jaderborg (Lindsborg: *News-Record,*1969).

69 Emory Lindquist, *Bethany in Kansas: The History of a College* (Lindsborg: Bethany College, 1975).

70 Doris L. Spong, "Alma Lind Swensson," *The Heritage of Augustana: Essays on the Life and Legacy of the Augustana Lutheran Church,* Hartland H. Gifford and Arland J. Hultgren, ed. (Minneapolis: Kirk House Publishers, 2004)

71 Maria Erling and Mark Granquist, *The Augustana Story: Shaping Lutheran Identity in North America* (Minneapolis, Minnesota: Augsburg Fortress, 2008). It was almost thirty years before American women had the right to vote; not until 1951 could women serve as trustees of their local congregation.

72 Carl Swensson, *Again in Sweden: Sketches and Reminiscences from the Land of Our Forefathers* (Lindsborg: Hemlandet, 1897). Originally published in Swedish.

73 Emory Lindquist, *Birger Sandzén: An Illustrated Biorgraphy* (Lawrence: University Press of Kansas, The Birger Sandzén Memorial Foundation, 1993).

74 Carl Swensson, A*gain in Sweden: Sketches and Reminiscences from the Land of Our Forefathers* (Lindsborg: Hemlandet,1897). Originally published in Swedish.

75 In American Scandinavian communities, one often hears the story of a husband and wife appearing before the judge in a divorce court. "He never says he loves me," the wife says to the judge. The husband turns to the judge and says, "I told her once that I loved her and if I change my mind, I'd let her know." This toast, perhaps, was Carl's public way of affection.

76 Carl Swensson, *Again in Sweden: Sketches and Reminiscences from the Land of Our Forefathers* (Lindsborg: Hemlandet,1897). Originally published in Swedish.

77 Ibid.

78 Carl Swensson, *Again in Sweden: Sketches and Reminiscences from the Land of Our Forefathers* (Lindsborg: Hemlandet, 1897). Originally published in Swedish.

79 Lindsborg *News* (March 23, 1900).

80 Charles Harger, "Singing Messiah on the Plains," *Ladies Home Journal,* volume 17, number 5 (April 1900).

81 Letter from Alma to Carl (May 1, 1882). Translated from the Swedish.

82 Letter from Alma to Carl (October 5). No year is given. Translated from the Swedish

83 Letter from Alma to Carl (February 22). No year is given. Translated from the Swedish

84 Letter from Alma to Carl (February 21, 1882). Translated from the Swedish.

85 Letter from Alma to Carl (October 5). No year is given in this letter. Translated from the Swedish.

86 Letter from Carl to Alma (October 22, 1901).

87 Letter from Carl to Alma (February 15, 1901).

88 Letter from Carl to Alma (April 26, 1901).

89 Emory Lindquist, *Smoky Valley People: A History of Lindsborg, Kansas* (1953).

90 Letter to Alma Swensson from Carl Swensson (October 6, 1901), trans. Charles W. Humphry, 2011, Bethany College Archives.

91 *New York Times* (October 21, 1901).

92 Lindsborg *Record* (November 16, 1901).

93 Remembered by Mrs. Carl Anderson, Bethany Lutheran Church Archives.

94 Lindsborg *Record* (November 16, 1901), here and below.

95 Emory Lindquist, *Birger Sandzén: An Illustrated Biorgraphy* (Lawrence: University Press of Kansas, The Birger Sandzén Memorial Foundation, 1993).

96 Lindsborg *Record* (November 16, 1901).

97 Ibid.

98   *New York Times* (March 29, 1903).

99   Interview with Ann Thorson Walton, Boberg scholar and author of *Ferdinand Bo-berg-Architect: The Complete Work* (Cambridge, Massachusetts: MIT Press, 1993).

100 The 1874 church, like many of its time, had the altar and pulpit as one, an American concept.

101 Letter to Alma Swensson from Carl Swensson, Omaha, Nebraska (December 9, 1903). The organ was placed in front, to the left of the altar, making it easily possible for the organist to watch the pastor as she led the congregational singing. The choir could be seated to the right of the organist.

102 Max Muller, *Prairie Carnegie* (Lindsborg: Quivira Press, 1977).

103 Letter from Lottie Swenson to Alma Swensson (February 12, 1904), Bethany College Archives.

104 Here and above, Lindsborg *Record* (February 26, 1904).

105 Ibid.

106 Ibid.

107 Lindsborg *News* (June 10, 1904).

108 Lindsborg *Record* (December 30, 1904).

109 Emory Lindquist, B*ethany in Kansas: the History of a College* (Lindsborg: Bethany College Publications, 1975).

110 Lindsborg *Record* (May 17 1907). The house is located at 343 First Street, formerly called College Street.

111 Letter to Mr. and Mrs. Wes Fisk from Elinor Lind Gahnstrom, niece of Alma Lind Swensson.

112 Lindsborg *Record* (July 5, 1907).

113 Ibid.

114 Minutes of the Lindsborg Cemetery Company, translated from Swedish by Charlotte Ternstrom.

115 Letter from Elinor Lind Gahnstrom to Mrs. Oman (February 11, 1987).

116 Gahnstrom letter to Mrs. Oman.

117 Gahnstrom to Mrs. Oman (February 11, 1987).

118 For further information, see Lennart Johnsson's essay, The Global Impact of Emmy Evald and the Women's Missionary Society, copyright 2006. Available online at www.augustanaheritage.org.

119 Mathilda Peterson, *These Fifty Years, 1892-1942* (Chicago: Women's Missionary Society of the Augustana Synod, 1942).

120 Ibid.

121 The English section was not a mere translation of the Swedish section. Both sections contained unique information—perhaps in recognition that many readers were bilingual.

122 Virginia P. Follstad, *The Augustana Evangelical Lutheran Church in Print* (ATLA Bibliography Series, 2007).

123 Mathilda Peterson, *These Fifty Years, 1892-1942* (Chicago: Women's Missionary Society of the Augustana Synod, 1942).

124 *Missions-Tidning* (August-September, 1919).

125 *Missions-Tidning* (May, 1924).

126 During Alma's lifetime, the *Messiah* was also presented in Wichita, Kansas City, and Oklahoma City.

127 *New York Times* (November 12, 1922).

128 In 1884, P. T. Lindholm was appointed director, followed by N.A. Krantz, Victor Lund, Vilhelm Lindberg, Sigfrid Laurin, Samuel Thorstenberg, Earl Rosenberg, H. E. Malloy, Hagbard Brasé, Arvid Wallin, Ralph Harrel, Rolf Espeseth, Eugene Pearson, Lloyd Speark, Elmer Copley, Greg Aune, Joel Panciera, Daniel Mahraun, Jeffrey Wall.

129 *New York Times* (April 12, 1935).

130 *New York Times* (February 4, 1923).

131 Lindsborg *News Record* (March 30, 1930).

132 *Missions-Tidning* (January, 1938).

133 Lindsborg *News Record* (February 9, 1939).

134 *Missions-Tidning* (July, 1939).

135 *Missions-Tidning* (January 1940). Translated by Charles W. Humphrey.

136 The tablet was fastened on a boulder brought from Twin Mounds, thirteen miles south of Lindsborg. A dedication service was held in the summer of 1941.

137 *Missions-Tidning* (January 1940). Translated from Swedish by Charles W. Humphrey.

138 Max Muller, *Prairie Carnegie* (Lindsborg: Quivira Press, 1977). The November 30, 1939, concert was Björling's second in Lindsborg. He came as a young boy with his family in 1920.

139 *Missions-Tidning* (January, 1940).

140 Ernst Pihlblad papers, Bethany College Archives.

141 Lindsborg *News Record* (January 18, 1940.).

142 See Glenda Riley, *The Female Frontier: A Comparative View of Women on the Prairie and the Plains* (Lawrence: Universtiy of Kansas Press, 1988), and Sandra L. Myres, Westering Women and the Frontier Experience 1800-1915 (Albuquerque: University of New Mexico Press, 1982).

143 Joel W. Lundeen, "Sweden," *Hymnal Companion to the Lutheran Book of Worship*, Marilyn Kay Stulken (Philadelphia: Fortress Press, 1981).

144 Sigrid Johnson is a member of the music faculty at St. Olaf College, Northfield, Minnesota, and directs the 100 voices of the Manitou Singers. She has prepared choirs for a host of internationally renowned conductors, including Neeme Jarvi,

Sir Neville Marriner, David Zinman, Leonard Slatkin, Gerard Schwarz. She is the associate conductor of VocalEssence and a featured lecturer for world symposiums of choral music in Copenhagen and Argentina.

145   Dr. Ernst Pihlblad papers, Bethany College Archives.

146   Sandra L. Myres, *Westering Women and the Frontier Experience 1800-1915* (Albuquerque: University of New Mexico Press, 1982).

147   *Time* magazine (Monday, December 16, 1935).

148   Gloria Cunningham, Lois Okerstrom, Helen Erickson, Martha Fosse, ed., *Touched by the African Soul* (Hillsboro: Partnership Book Services, 1998).

149   The Augustana Synod merged with the United Lutheran Church in America, the American Evangelical Lutheran Church, and the Suomi Synod in 1962 to create the Lutheran Church in America (LCA). In 1970, the LCA approved the ordination of women.

150   Ginger cookies.

151   *Till minne af . . .* (To the Memory of . . .)

152   The Oratorio Society has sung *Passion of Our Lord According to Saint Matthew* on Good Friday since 1925.

153   Dag Hammarskjöld, *Markings* (New York: Alfred A. Knopf, 1970).

Index

103, 104, 105, 106, 107, 110, 111, 112, 113, 115, 116, 118, 119, 120, 121

Swensson, Anna 40, 118

Swensson, Annie 29, 33, 41, 42, 44, 46, 58, 62, 69, 70, 73, 79, 81, 95, 96, 97, 98, 106

Swensson, Bertha 41, 42, 44, 46, 50, 58, 62, 63, 69, 70, 72, 73, 79, 80, 81, 98, 106

Swensson, Carl Aaron 7, 8, 9, 10, 11, 16, 19, 20, 23, 24, 27, 28, 29, 30, 31, 32, 33, 34, 35, 36, 37, 38, 41, 42, 43, 44, 45, 46, 47, 48, 49, 50, 51, 52, 53, 54, 55, 56, 57, 58, 59, 61, 62, 63, 64, 65, 66, 67, 68, 69, 70, 71, 72, 73, 74, 76, 78, 79, 80, 81, 82, 83, 90, 95, 96, 97, 98, 99, 101, 106, 107, 110, 118, 119, 120

Swensson, John 53

Swensson, Jonas 15, 50, 115

Swensson, Luther 53, 97

Swensson, Maria Blixt 41

Sydhoff, Beate 110

Talley, Marian 89

Thomas, W. W. 57, 64, 76

Thorstenberg 46, 47, 48, 54, 73, 121

Tourel, Jennie 89

Ucko, Hans 110

Udden, J. A. 35, 89, 90

Uppsala 36, 50, 51, 106, 109

Vanaberg, Martin 111

Värmland 21, 23, 24, 110, 116

Västergötland 9, 25, 35, 43

Vestling, Axel 79

von Schéele, Anna Gustafva Maria 59

von Schéele, Knut Henning Gauzelius 59, 60, 61, 62, 63, 64, 70

Wennstam, Thomas A. 110

Wergeland, Agnes Mathilde 11

Wetterstrom, Mrs. Hjalmer 100

Women's Missionary Society 44, 45, 46, 53, 55, 68, 69, 73, 74, 76, 77, 81, 85, 86, 87, 93, 94, 96, 97, 105, 106, 120, 121

World War I 89

Ysaÿe, Eugène 89

Zimbalist, Efrem 89

Zorn, Anders 43, 48, 50

Zorngården 50